Remembering

Craven County

Remembering Craven County

TALES OF TARHEEL HISTORY

Bill Hand

THE History PRESS

Published by The History Press
Charleston, SC 29403
www.historypress.net

Cover image courtesy of Tryon Palace Historic Sites and Gardens.

First published 2006

Manufactured in the United States

ISBN 1.59629.157.7

Library of Congress Cataloging-in-Publication Data

Hand, Bill, 1956-
Remembering Craven County : tales of Tarheel history / Bill Hand.
p. cm.
ISBN 1-59629-157-7 (alk. paper)
1. Craven County (N.C.)--History--Anecdotes. 2. Craven County (N.C.)--Biography--Anecdotes. 3. New Bern (N.C.)--History--Anecdotes. 4. New Bern (N.C.)--Biography--Anecdotes. I. Title.
F262.C8H36 2006
975.6'192--dc22
2006018715

For Sara and Rachel, wonderful daughters…
there will be a test!

CONTENTS

Introduction

"It ought never to be forgotten that the past is the parent of the present."
—John C. Calhoun

Welcome to a look at the parents of New Bern's past. We are much more than a couple of rivers, a lot of carved and sculpted bears and a collection of quaint restaurants and shops.

We're *history*.

More exactly, we're the sum total of the people of our past.

We flow from a stream of interrelated individuals and events that give our town a unique and vital flavor. Of these visitors and residents, some are well known today; others were famous only in their time; still others were celebrities only to their neighbors and the loved ones in their homes. But all were influential in making us who we are today.

And that's what this book is all about: people and their interrelations.

So, as you are reading, don't be surprised when you come upon a piece of information that gives you a sense of *déjà vu*. One of the primary themes of this book is how so many of these people and events interrelate: by blood, by friendship, by shared places or common events. How do the Sisters of Mercy, George Washington, a Confederate general and a man who shot down a governor relate? What is the common thread between a Catholic judge, a Protestant patriot doctor and a possibly counterfeiting printer?

These are the shades of Craven County—not only ghostly shades, but also the shadows and variations of our city's lineage.

Of course a book like this took a lot of assistance.

I would like to thank Dick Lore, the excellent New Bern historian, and Andrew Duppstadt, Civil War historian extraordinaire, for reading this compilation and helping to make sense of it.

At first a federal building and a library, City Hall in New Bern overlooks a marker for James Davis (the colony's first printer), the bust of Christopher de Graffenried and the original office of Judge William Gaston. *Picture by the author.*

New Bern is blessed with historical records and the talented people who know how to access them. I have to show my gratitude to John Leys, John Green and the Kellenberger Room at the New Bern Public Library and especially Dean Knight, custodian of the ancient and historical volumes at Tryon Palace Historic Sites and Gardens.

I owe kudos to other Palace folks: Nancy Hawley, Shirley Willis and Kay Williams.

The New Bern Historical Society under Newsom Williams was also of much assistance.

Then, of course, there is my family: my wife, Roberta, who proofed and encouraged, the girls who tolerate my endless devotion to things past (the eighties is a past ancient enough for them) and the obsessive dog who stayed out of my lap long enough to let me type those blessed words, "The End."

Part I

The Colonial Period

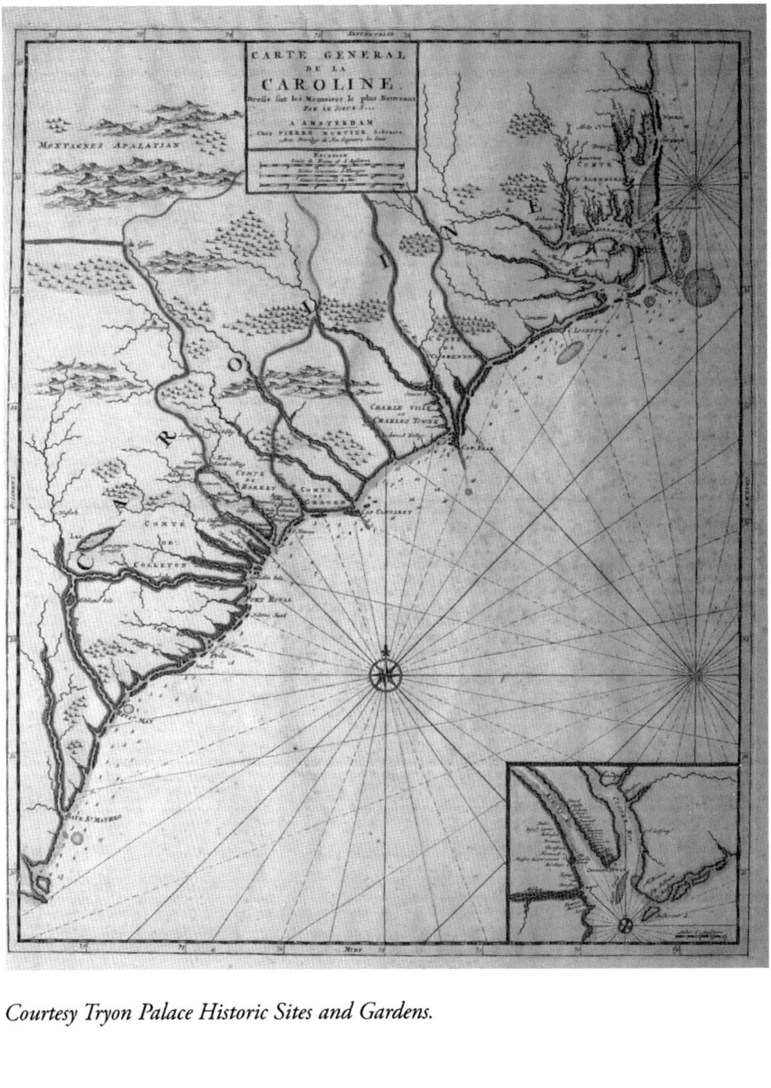

Courtesy Tryon Palace Historic Sites and Gardens.

Before the Swiss: The Tuscarora Who Ran the Town

Before a bewigged Swiss Baron or an English writer and explorer tramped our sandy banks, New Bern was an Indian town. Chatooka (or one of many other spellings) was its name. It means "Where the Fish are Drawn Out," which gives you an idea of the main work down here before 1710. (Hint: it probably had nothing to do with herding buffaloes.)

More specifically, Chatooka was a village of the Neusoic Indians, a branch of the Tuscarora tribe. Like many Native American tribes, their ways were very unfamiliar and unpredictable to the new settlers. For example, they sold and vacated their town for Baron de Graffenried's benefit and later joined the fight that filled his town's environs with six-foot-deep holes, each one labeled "Rest In Peace."

We have a few sources on what these folks were like: the best is John Lawson's *A New Voyage to Carolina*, published back in 1709. He'd spent some time living near this village at the creek that bears his name and shared his house with a member of the tribe.

Lawson described the Indians as "well-shap'd clean-made People… chiefly inclined to be tall. They are a very streight People, and never bend forwards, or stoop in the Shoulders, unless much power'd by old Age. Their limbs are exceeding well-shap'd." Their eyes were black or hazel, their skin "tawny, which would not be so dark, did they not dawb themselves with Bears Oil."

The Indians were particular about their hair, greasing it down (which was why baldness was so rare among them, Lawson suspected). "Some of the Indians wear great Bobs in their Ears," Lawson mentioned of their fashion sense, "and sometimes in the Holes thereof they put Eagles and other Birds, Feathers, for a Trophy. When they kill any Fowl, they commonly pluck off the downy Feathers, and

Council Bluff on the Neuse River: the traditional spot where Baron deGraffenried purchased New Bern from King Taylor. *Photo by the author.*

stick them all over their Heads." It must have been entertaining to watch a violent sneeze.

Both men and women wore bracelets of brass and necklaces of shells, which they used as money.

As to families, the men hunted and fought—the Tuscarora were noticeably warlike—and the women farmed, cooked, raised the kids, served as runners between villages and carried firewood, bark and other loads. Children were named at birth, although never in honor of a parent. If a girl got an awful name, she was just stuck. But a boy who was named something undesirable was in luck: when he became a warrior at sixteen or seventeen he chose a name for himself, usually that of an animal such as "Panther" or "Alligator."

The town was run by a hereditary king. The quirk here is that his son could never take his place. After all, given the possibility of "sins of the flesh," there was no absolute guarantee that the king was really the father of his wife's child. One could not guarantee that child's blood lineage. Not so with the king's sister: if she had a baby, it was obviously hers, so her son was heir to the throne. When an heir was judged truly bad, there was a fair chance his uncle would poison him, clearing the way for some better man next in line. It was not so different from medieval Europe!

The king's rule was not absolute; he had a council of war captains and others, all the eldest of the village, who would carefully discuss and debate every issue from war and trade to social services. Solutions were almost always reached by majority vote.

They ate what was hunted, gathered, fished or grown in small plots. Wasp larvae were considered quite the gourmet treat. Cornbread was a staple, and cornmeal was prepared by several women or girls beating away with pestles in a long mortar.

They hunted in large groups, sometimes wandering days from home, after the leaves fell and dried. They enjoyed setting fire to the woods as a mean of driving the animals into "small Necks of Land and Isthmus's, where they kill and destroy what they please." As you might imagine, this caused quite a bit of trouble when a European settler's farm or plantation was in the fire's way.

Lawson described them using a curious match, six feet long and made of a black moss (perhaps Spanish moss) that hung off the trees. One can imagine how awkward this matchbook would have been, but Lawson vowed, once dried, that the moss worked better than anything the Europeans had.

In religion, they accepted a god who created all things and allowed for a devil who was responsible for most of the evil. Like many tribes and the ancient Europeans, the Tuscarora had their wealth of mythology and creation tales.

Indian doctors were very powerful men, and Lawson vowed he saw them cure many things no white man could.

To one another, they were loving and tolerant. "They know not what Jealousy is," Lawson wrote. "They are very bashful, especially the young Maids…I never saw a Scold amongst them, and to their Children they are extraordinary tender and indulgent." They assisted their poor, treated the elderly with deep respect and honored their dead with a devotion we would consider macabre.

While generous to their own, they were not so pleasant to their foes. Slaves (usually taken from other tribes) started their servitude by getting the front half of their foot cut off (such hobbling made escape difficult), though they were not overworked once they healed. Men sentenced to die for crimes were tortured in hideous ways, for a quick death was considered too honorable. Enemies, too, were abused both before and after death, as too many colonists would find out in the Tuscarora War of 1711.

Lawson would describe the Indians as better than Europeans in many ways. They were shamefully abused, he wrote, in trade, encroachment and through slavery. Lawson was concerned enough about them that he wrote an extensive plan to evangelize the Tuscarora. Usually, missionary work among Indians was nearly non-existent in the southern climes, which were mostly settled as commercial ventures.

Lawson added a dire warning: though "the freest People from Heats and Passions which possess the *Europeans*," he wrote, "the *Indians* are very revengeful, and never forget an Injury done, till they have receiv'd Satisfaction."

It was a lesson, to the chagrin of many, that would be learned too late.

The Early Life of Christopher de Graffenried: Playboy of the Swiss World

Baron Christopher de Graffenried's history as the founder of New Bern is well known, but his early life is particularly interesting—especially as a means of understanding what happened once he got here.

Born to a wealthy and titled Swiss miser, Christopher would become the idol of European courts, the heartthrob of several girls and a spendthrift perpetually in debt. He would carry many titles throughout his life, some of them—Governor of Yverton and Lord of Worb—sounding like distinctions one of Tolkein's hobbits or elves might covet.

De Graffenried was the son of the heavily titled Anton of Bern, one of those quiet, bookish types for whom "extravagance and unnecessary expenditure was unknown," according to one family historian. In contrast, his eldest son Christopher was high-strung and hardly able to sit still. In the present-day, supra-medicated world he might have been treated for attention deficit disorder.

At seven, the over lively Christopher was sent to a severe schoolmaster who required every word spoken in class to be in Latin. Christopher found the experience to be *infelicitas extremus* and, after seven years of Dickensian hard knocks, he fled the school and took up with relatives.

Not long after, Anton began negotiations to purchase a salt mine and Christopher became smitten with the salt mine manager's daughter. Anton tried to include her in his arrangements, but when the deal fell through, so did the damsel.

Christopher's was becoming a Charlie Brown life: his uncle, captain of the guard for the Prince of Saxony, was certain he could land him a position in the prince's court. Unfortunately, the uncle died as did the position.

A bust of Baron de Graffenried, from downtown New Bern. *Photo by the author.*

Christopher began to hanker for the joys of the road. In 1679, at age eighteen, his father sent him to Heidelberg for studies; distrustful of his son's financial acumen, Anton placed Christopher's funds under the control of a theology student there. Christopher neglected his studies and partied with the royal court. He made quite a splash by getting himself into a duel. The splash was felt by an angry father, who hauled him back home.

For the next few years the young man meandered from one school to another, all the while pleading to be sent to London until his father finally gave in. Anton had hoped a letter of introduction would save him money by convincing the courts to lavish his near-penniless son with their own. Unfortunately for Christopher, the man who was to receive the letter and do the lavishing turned out to be in debtor's prison.

Christopher had a moderate sum of money in the form of an inheritance from his late mother, a small portion of which Anton reluctantly sent. Between this and his own charismatic nature, Christopher quickly rose in English society and in the eyes of King Charles II himself.

Soon he was in love again, this time with the niece of the Duke of Buckingham. She was of high birth but little money, and to land her he would need a title and funds. Casting about, he decided to purchase a lucrative commission in the army. It would cost one thousand pounds, but Christopher had ten times that amount left in his mother's will. Forgetting his well-placed fear of his father, he wrote home demanding the money. Anton, having heard exaggerated rumors of his son's misbehavior, responded by demanding he come back to the continent, threatening to revoke his hereditary rights if he didn't return. Stuck, Christopher went back with his tail between his legs.

Christopher then spent a few good years in Paris, where he met the Sun King himself and became a veritable Benjamin Franklin with the court ladies. But in 1683, the twenty-three-year-old Christopher was summoned again to the dull air of home and his father's angry lectures regarding his spendthrift ways. Anton also introduced him to his bride. This was an age, remember, when marriages of romance were more common in a Moliére play than in a titled man's household. The bride was nineteen-year-old Regina Tscharner who was well bred, good-looking and of limited income.

Eventually they would grow close, though at first Christopher was probably not pleased. Adding insult, his father forced Christopher to loan him the money to buy his wedding gift.

They lived together in relative obscurity until his forty-first year, when he became governor of Yverton. He hoped this would give him the financial comfort for which he yearned, but the expensive parties he felt obliged to host ate up much of his new income. Religious problems forced him to keep an expensive garrison and, while other governors made up the difference by over-tithing their subjects, de Graffenried could not bring himself to abuse them. Despairing, he began to read about a wealth of silver mines to be had in the English-controlled New World and, like a conquistador at mid-life, his debt-blurred eyes grew hopeful and wide.

In England, Christopher met the Carolinian explorer John Lawson, who convinced him to buy several thousand acres of land at the confluence of the Trent and Neuse rivers. Queen Anne, anxious to settle a growing population of palatine refugees, happily paid for the passage of some several hundred settlers to the new land (about half would die en route), while Christopher himself brought about one hundred Swiss. By the fall of 1710, New Bern began.

Of course, North Carolina had no more silver mines than Florida had fountains of youth; embroiled in politics, destitution, ill luck and a nasty Indian war, de Graffenried's settlement was far from successful: it barely survived. Leaving his eldest son behind, Christopher fled Columbia's golden shores broke, broken and so disgraced that he arrived in Bern under an assumed name. He would spend much of the rest of his life trying to explain away his part in the whole affair.

Fortunately, despite a rough beginning, New Bern would find a much brighter future than her founding father.

John Lawson:
Death of a Renaissance Man

It is hard to come up with something Lawson did not do well. He was an explorer, writer, dedicated botanist, mapmaker and surveyor who laid out and helped found two towns; he was also an advocate for the better treatment of the local Indians. Though he apparently had a common-law wife, his writing suggests that he had strong religious feelings as well: in his book, *A New Voyage to Carolina*, he outlines a plan of missions outreach to the Indians.

He was an Englishman, probably a gentleman, who in 1700 was staring down the expanse of a new century. Desiring adventure, he bumped into a fellow who "was very well acquainted with the Ways of Living in both *Indies;* of whom, having made Enquiry concerning them, he assur'd me, that *Carolina* was the best Country I could go to." He wasted no time in boarding a ship for the New World.

After a brief stop in Dutch-heavy New York City, he sailed past the barren wild Outer Banks into the civilized harbor of Charles Town, South Carolina.

Had he been a less restless man, he might have settled in that beautiful place, and perhaps you would read his story in some quaint Charlestonian history. John had an urge to travel, however, and that urge conveniently converged with the Lords Proprietors, who had received huge strips of American land from King Charles in exchange for their past support. Most of these proprietors were absentee landlords living in England, and they desired a map of their distant claim. They contracted him, and on December 28, 1700, John Lawson, with five Englishmen, three Indian men and an Indian wife, set out for the Santee River in a big canoe.

The fifty-nine-day adventure would cover roughly 550 miles. He would meet a seven-foot Indian warrior and a noseless Santee chief. Keeping copious notes, John would not only record the geography of this land for his bosses but would also describe dozens of animals and

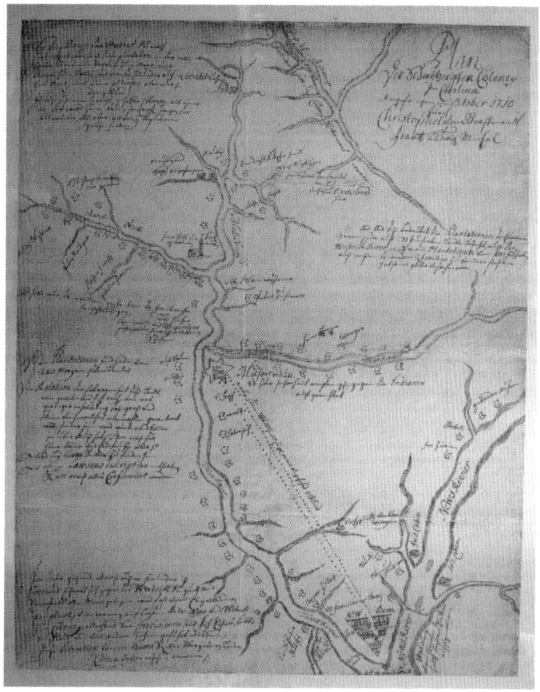

John Lawson's design for the town of New Bern in 1710. *Courtesy Tryon Palace Historic Sites and Gardens.*

plants in detail. Lawson compiled one of our best early studies on the society of the Santee and Tuscarora Indians.

He ended his travels at the English settlements on the "Pampticough River" near present-day Washington, North Carolina. He liked the people and the region, and so he settled in.

Over the next few years he would attempt to help settle contentious disputes over the Virginia boundary line, and in 1705, laid out the town of Bath, where he would purchase a pair of fine lots near the river. There he would pen his book and meet his "Dearly beloved Hannah Smith," with whom he would live and father a daughter, Isabella (who was no more than nine when he died).

At some point, he found time to live among the Indians of Chatooka on the Neuse and Trent Rivers. He built himself a house along a creek that now bears his name, sharing it with an Indian, a bulldog and—not his choice—a booming-voiced, nesting alligator.

He must have admired this little peninsula between two rivers, for in 1710 he would convince Christopher de Graffenried to purchase the land and settle it. Somewhere during all this, he also spent a fair amount of time conversing with James Petiver, a London apothecary who was a huge collector of plants. Lawson often sent specimens to him, and when he sailed for London he carried a few.

In 1709 he sailed for England, bringing his newly drawn maps and reports to the proprietors and, more importantly for historians, the manuscript of his very fine book. Petiver, who had a reputation as one of the best botanists of his day, wrote a letter of introduction for John while he was there. In it, he said that Lawson "is very a cautious person and hath lately treated the Quadrupeds, Birds, Fishes, Reptiles & Vegitables, particularly the Trees, with a great deal of Judgment and accuracy."

To fast-forward: Lawson met de Graffenried in London, where the latter was seeking a method to transport a number of Palatines and Swiss Anabaptists to a colony in the New World. Lawson sold him on the little peninsula on the Neuse and Trent Rivers, for which de Graffenried paid the Proprietors, the Indians and Lawson.

In 1710 the colony of New Bern began and, although it got off to a rocky start, everyone thought things were beginning to go just fine.

Then, in September 1711, the Tuscarora launched a surprise attack and massacred nearly two hundred people in one day. The causes of this war were many: among them, the Indians were angry at being continually cheated by traders and seeing their people kidnapped and sold off as slaves. European encroachment was the major issue—and the settlement of New Bern, apparently, was a big part of that rub.

Historians consider John the attack's first victim. Several days before the attacks, he and de Graffenried were captured and tried by the Tuscarora. According to de Graffenried, Lawson was executed in a most painful way.

De Graffenried was freed, due in part to a threat from Virginia governor Alexander Spotswood. He would complain bitterly in his own book about how unpleasant a man Lawson was, but the book was so vituperative in assigning fault that one is tempted to take it with a cup of salt.

Why *did* the Tuscarora begin a war by killing the man who seemed to be the closest friend they had? It is one of the great ironies of our history for which no definitive answer has been found.

Lawson left a young daughter, a woman he loved, a fascinating book and a great legacy behind.

Arthur Dobbs: The Venus Flytrap Man

He would never be as famous or admired as his successor, William Tryon, but this curious colonial governor would leave a mark by which we should remember him. He was the first European to report the finding of a curious plant known mainly to North Carolina's coastal forests, especially in Craven County's own Croatan.

Arthur Dobbs had spent most of his life in and around Carrickfergus—a town you hope you never have to say three times fast—in Northern Ireland. There, he was a politician in parliament and a member of Jonathan Swift's very tiny congregation. Swift, being an ultra-Irish nationalist and Dobbs, being more levelheaded with the British, were often at political loggerheads.

Dobbs had a number of curious fancies, not the least of which was a quixotic obsession with finding a northwest passage around North America. He was, in fact, a driving force behind a major exploration in 1741 of the Hudson Bay. Christopher Middleton, the leader of the expedition, found nothing of course, and Dobbs would spend much of what was left of his life accusing Middleton and the Hudson Bay Company of intentionally hiding the passage he was so sure was there.

Dobbs was also a botanist, continually experimenting and studying plants, birds and bees. He was especially stung by a love of the honey-gathering fellows, chasing them about the fields with a magnifying glass in his hand. He is actually credited with a major discovery about pollination when he observed that the bees transferred pollen from the anthers of one flower to the pistil of a kindred one. No one had observed this role of the honeybees before—at least no one had written it out in an official paper. Dobbs also drew accurate observations as to why bees are so intent on building hexagonal honeycomb cells, which I would love to explain to you if I could make heads or tails of what he wrote.

Dobbs was drawn to a career in North Carolina at least in part because he had purchased a huge amount of settlement land near present-day Charlotte. His activities in science and government had made him popular in London, and in 1752, when the aged Gabriel Johnston died, Dobbs was named to replace him as governor of North Carolina. On October 31, 1754, he arrived in New Bern and was sworn in. He was sixty-five then—an age when most men are wrapping up, rather than beginning, their careers.

He would govern for ten years, with his primary political legacy that of leading the colony successfully through the French and Indian War. For a man of his age he was healthy, but the climate of New Bern was more than his rheumatism could take. He bought land overlooking the Neuse River farther inland, toward present-day Kinston, in an area he named Tower Hill. He convinced the assembly to accept that as the capital, they turned around and wrote London with a list of reasons why they actually opposed it and the Crown told him Tower Hill would never be. Still holding a craven dislike for New Bern, he pulled his base of operations to Brunswick and Wilmington, near the South Carolina border. To keep the coastal powers happy (the inland was only then beginning to be settled), he kept rotating government sessions from Wilmington to New Bern to Edenton.

The latter years of his governorship were not happy: the end of the French and Indian War meant that the assemblymen no longer had to get along to stay alive, and they seemed to fight each other and Dobbs at every turn. As if he felt he had a need to make himself a target of ridicule, he married a sixteen-year-old girl named Justina Davis. The result was mockery (and possibly envy) among North Carolinian men. Whether such a young bride improved his health or hastened his end is anyone's guess.

It was midway through his governorship, in 1760, that Dobbs's old botanist roots were reawakened by a fascinating plant. Surviving on meat as much as sunlight, the Venus Flytrap had been growing, nameless and elusive, in the North Carolina woods for eons. We do not know if he found it himself or whether someone knowing his penchant for curious specimens brought it to him. Either way, he was enthralled.

Botanical historians describe Dobbs as a "Puritan botanist." I am not sure what that means, but this "Puritan" with a magnifying glass may have had his mind in the proverbial gutter when he named the plant after the goddess of love. "It is unclear if this was in reference to the plant's ability to trap, or ensnare, insects as the goddess Venus empowered women with the ability to ensnare men, or because some people claim the traps resemble certain aspects of female anatomy," writes Wayne Schmidt in a web essay of the carnivorous plant.

Dobbs's discovery—a meat-eating plant whose bizarreness might not be equaled again until the discovery of the transmammalian platypus in 1797—became a sensation.

Although his replacement, William Tryon, arrived in October 1764, Dobbs decided to wait until spring to sail home to Ireland. He fell ill in late March but still insisted on packing up his books in preparation for the trip. His doctor felt this to be seriously unwise: as Tryon would write, "His physician had no other means to prevent his fatiguing himself, than by telling him he had better prepare himself for a much longer voyage."

The longer one came. The discoverer of both the Venus Flytrap and the cosmic purpose of the honeybee died on March 28, 1765. "I have lost one of the best and tenderest of husbands and you a kind and most affectionate father," Justina would write to her stepson (who was significantly older than she).

The late governor of North Carolina's funeral service was performed by a justice of the peace, as no clergyman could be found. He was buried in Brunswick, a town that, like him, would fade from existence in a few short years. His exact gravesite is unknown.

But at least some beekeepers and plant fanciers know who he was.

George Whitefield: New Bern's Great Awakening

George Washington slept here.

But George Whitefield did, too.

You know Mr. Whitefield: the famous evangelist of the Great Awakening. He was as popular a celebrity then, as Billy Graham is today.

Whitefield, stout and bewigged, was an Englishman of some influence and power. He was known for a booming voice that could be heard over large crowds. More often than not, he spoke in fields, for there weren't a lot of buildings that could hold the listeners he drew. He was sometimes called the "prince of pulpit orators," which probably pleased him, and also "Doctor Squintum," which probably did not. The latter moniker was a result of his strabismus, a condition in which both of his eyes could not focus on the same subject. "He was afflicted with a squint so severe that no one knew exactly where (or at whom) he was looking," one biographer said. One wonders if he could have made it in today's image-crazy world.

He traveled America seven times, visiting churches from Boston to Savannah, where he had founded an orphanage. His comings and goings were fodder for the press. Even James Davis, the official printer of North Carolina in the colonial days, lauded his tours: "He has been assiduous in his Labours among us, notwithstanding his bodily Infirmities; and…he still appears to be influenced, in his general Design, by a benevolent Disposition toward Mankind," Davis reported in 1764.

His first visitation to New Bern was in 1739, when he was just thirty-six, a spry young man with a disturbing gaze. This was also his first trip to America. On that call, he gave a Christmas day sermon at the Court House (the church had not been built yet). It was not the most propitious of visits. While his listeners were

This outdoor chapel is built on the foundations of the original Christ's Church in which Whitefield spoke. *Photo by the author.*

"uncommonly attentive, and most were driven to tears," he would confide to his journal, he "mourned much in spirit, to see in what an indifferent manner everything was carried on." He saw the presence of a dancing-master as the purest evidence of the town's carnality. Shocked, he added that even the minister "Countenance[d] a dancing-master, by suffering his own son to be one of his learners... Such sinful entertainments enervate the minds of the people, and insensibly lead them into effeminacy and ruin."

So much for *Dancing with the Stars.*

Still, he was not ready to write New Bern off. In 1764, he visited again. By now he was sixty-one and growing infirm. New Bern may have still had its dancing-masters, but the town was under tighter spiritual control. James Reed, missionary for the Society for the Propagation of the Gospel, ran the church now. A man with a heart for God's service and the people of the colony, he was also a man who was careful to protect the rights and reputations of his fellow pastors. He knew Whitefield's reputed ties with the highly emotional form of worship of the Methodists. Besides, Whitefield had a reputation for "enthusiastic ranting." Reed was concerned that the old fellow would stir up the "enthusiasts" and non-conformist believers bringing embarrassment and trouble for the more staid Anglicans in town.

Reed could not be in town the day he arrived, but he assigned a vestryman to keep a wary eye on their guest. Aware of the home pastor's views, Whitefield told the vestryman plainly that he did not support the enthusiasts or most of their views. Reed, however, was not totally convinced. "Granting they were not his immediate disciples and followers I do affirm," he wrote, but, "they sprung from the seed which he first planted in New England." There was also a "New Lights" doctrine going about that Reed feared Whitefield would promote: a belief that theology should be dispensed with. And what about other unorthodox beliefs? Would Whitefield preach against infant baptism? Would he demand the rebaptism of adults? This might seem minor today, but recall that this was 1764; it had not been so long since men were killed or imprisoned for such disagreements in Europe.

As it turned out, there was little to be concerned about. Whitefield had become a Calvinist in doctrine, opposing the key Wesleyan tenant of free will. He entered the new, pretty little Christ's Church in downtown New Bern in mid-November and delivered a sermon that pleased the "orthodox" believers.

"At New Bern, last Sunday," he told his journal in Brunswick. "Good impressions were made." With the colonists being "exceedingly desirous to hear the gospel," he added, he was "almost determined to come back early in the spring."

He did exactly that. Speaking first in Wilmington, where Governor William Tryon heard him with delight, he then delivered a sermon in New Bern that delighted Reverend Reed. "He arrived here on his return from the Southern Provinces on Thursday evening in Passion Week," Reed wrote the bishop. And, as "the People were very desirous to hear him I…offered him the reading desk and Pulpit on Good Friday." Good Friday didn't work because of a bout of asthma, but on Easter Sunday Whitefield delivered a powerful sermon that startled the enthusiasts. "His Sermon," Reverend Reed crowed, "was clear of enthusiastic Rant and really a good one the substance of it contradictory to the Tenets…of making…religion a mere Cloak as a pretext for…indolence and sloth. I must say his preaching has been of infinite service and I should be glad to see him more frequently provided he would always preach in the same strain."

But George Whitefield would not return. His health continued to fail, and in five years he passed away, full of service, having "finished the race." The dance-happy town with which he had so many concerns early on—and whose religious leaders would later have such concerns with *him*—would keep memories of him, rested in peace.

The Fall of Mr. Tomlinson: New Bern's First Schoolmaster

Spoiled children and their more spoiled parents are a story as old as education, I suppose. It is certainly a story as old as education in New Bern.

Born in 1732 in the parish of Thursby, England, a skip and a hop from Hadrian's Wall, Thomas Tomlinson was a boy who fell in love with learning. Studying hard at the Uldale Grammar School, he returned there to begin teaching at age 20 in 1752. A plaque in the little St. James Church there honors him today: "He taught… with so much credit to himself and satisfaction to his employers, as to leave few equals in his profession."

James Reed was looking for a good schoolmaster. The pious rector had convinced the assembly that New Bern needed a public school (to be run under the auspices of the Church of England) and it had agreed. But where to find a good schoolmaster in the colonies? New Bern had a number of men who hired themselves out privately for the trade, but none were truly qualified, in Reed's opinion. One of his parishioners, a planter, thought he had an idea: his brother back home who taught so well at the Uldale school.

The church contacted Tomlinson and, whether for love of adventure or a desire to be near his brother, the schoolmaster closed the doors of St. James behind him forever. Arriving in December 1763, he wasted no time: by January 1 he was teaching young scholars—"as many as he could instruct," Reed proclaimed.

The new school, which would eventually evolve into the New Bern Academy, instructed both girls and boys; its students included the children of the wealthy and influential as well as up to ten poor children, whose tuition would be covered by a fund overseen by the trustees.

A recreated eighteenth-century schoolroom, on display at Tryon Palace Historic Sites and Gardens. *Photo by the author.*

Reed was greatly enamored of him. "During eleven years Residence in this province I have not found any man so well qualified for the Care of a school," he would write. Mr. Tomlinson "has given great satisfaction to the Parents of such children as are under his care."

Thomas's students were fond of him as well. "Mr. Tomlinson keeps a good house and is pleasant and kind," one youth, who shared a house with the teacher, would write to a friend. "Mr. Tomlinson sees to it that we have our lessons done each evening and that is the only problem of living with a schoolmaster."

During his ten years as schoolmaster, he taught as many as eighty students who came from as far away as Wilmington. It wasn't long before an assistant schoolmaster had to be hired, and a Mr. Parrot was brought in. Tuition was twenty shillings per quarter, although Thomas rarely saw that money: the scholars' parents had a bad habit of neglecting to pay and would eventually be in arrears of as much as fifty pounds. Even with a stipend from the Society for the Propagation of the Gospel (SPG), his pay was low. Still, he seemed content. "He is the first person I verily believe that ever taught school in Newbern for any considerable time without complaining of bad pay and very loudly," Reed wrote, apparently remembering the private teachers of earlier days. "Such complaints I have seen nailed up at the Church Door."

Despite his obvious love for his students and his calling, Tomlinson was destined to fall; ironically (but not, perhaps, unusually) it was his devotion to education that brought him down.

The Colonial American student was not quite like the youth from his old Uldale parish days. Early on, he was warned that the parents in the colonies were overly indulgent of their youth: discipline could be a challenge. Thomas tried to be patient, using "every little artifice to avoid Severity" with his pupils. However, one student became so unruly that Thomas feared he was an endangerment to the other students. He expelled the child and made "some little difficulties about their Readmission."

It was Tomlinson's misfortune that this was the child of one of the school's most vindictive and powerful trustees. It "was like the Sin against the Holy Ghost, never to be forgiven," Reed wrote. The trustee and one or two of his cronies became "his most implacable enemies."

The trustee was obviously adept at politics. Bringing most of the other trustees (whom Thomas later described as tame and acquiescent) under his banner, he began holding meetings without notifying those members (such as Reed) who supported Tomlinson. When a new school in Wilmington drained the attendance at New Bern, Thomas asked the trustees to cover the cost of five additional needy students to raise funds. Citing low finances they refused, although according to Reed, the treasurer at that time had more than enough money to cover them. To add insult to injury, they revoked the tuition of the five needy students currently in the school.

Most parents still spoke highly of Mr. Tomlinson, but the trustees finally found someone—a fellow well in debt on his tuition—willing to accuse the schoolmaster of negligence. The trustees tried to use this to remove Thomas, though they never let him face his accuser. His job was offered to Mr. Parrot who, seeing the whole fiasco as a kangaroo court, refused and, being laid off, continued assisting Thomas as a volunteer.

Unable to fire him, the trustees finally resorted to stopping his pay. Suddenly without income, Thomas was forced to pressure all the parents-in-arrears to pay up. Instead, making rears of them*selves*, they ridiculed him in front of their children. Fed up, Tomlinson resigned.

Perhaps he was totally burned out on the whole idea of education: he left for New England where he lived for a while, but he did not return home to England. He eventually returned to New Bern to set up a successful mercantile business in town. He would marry a woman named Elizabeth and, by his death in 1802, own four slaves. He would be buried just inside the gate of the Cedar Grove Cemetery. Not forgetting his roots, he left a large endowment to the Uldale schools and the poor of Thursby Parish, still in use today.

His story is an interesting exception to the biblical maxim that "A prophet is not without honor, save in his own country."

The Perfect Storm: The Hurricane of 1769

If you have lived in this area long, you've probably come across those curious bits of precipitation we like to call "hurricanes." They are not very welcome visitors, but they *do* fulfill our need to complain to our relatives. We must be fond of them somehow; after all, since 1953 we've been giving them names.

Among New Bern's historic woes was a doozy of a hurricane, which wiped out a fair chunk of the town in September of 1769.

Governor William Tryon, then living in Brunswick, may have had some Shakespearean premonition of it in late August as he watched "a blazing Planet or star" whizzing through space. A modern man stuck on the portents of the past, he wondered if it might prophesy a future event.

Seven days later the hurricane wreaked havoc from Cape Fear to Williamsburg.

John Smith, a New Bern businessman, noted that rain had begun to fall about six o'clock p.m. on September 7. His record of the rising wind included an interesting description of the circular habits of a hurricane: "the wind [was] at N.E., and so continued until 9 or 10, then shifted to S.E. and about two in the morning the tide was 10 or 12 feet above its usual heighth; about this time the wind shifted to S.W. which occasioned the tide to fall, or it would have destroyed this town, which is already near effected."

New Bern is not exactly known for its high elevation: the rising storm surge quickly threatened lives and homes. Smith lived on the waterfront, and his house abutted that of the wealthy and powerful merchant, Samuel Cornell. Smith's cellar was stacked with wine, rum and sugar, and every item was "either stove to Pieces or floated away," New Bernian Thomas Howe would write.

This hurricane took place at the turn of the twentieth century, but it was hardly the first in the area. *Courtesy of the New Bern Historical Society.*

While his basement flooded and his stores disappeared, Smith stood above, listening to the growing trauma of the storm:

> *My dwelling-house, and Mr. Cornell's, which joins it, and stood on a stone wall 22 inches thick and near 9 feet from the surface of the earth, were almost washed down; the lower floors of both fell in, the other parts are miraculously standing on parts of the cellar wall; and all the furniture of both houses that were in the lower floors are broke to pieces and washed away, as also many others. At one in the morning the water was 18 inches on my lower floor. I broke through into Mr. Cornell's garret, with my wife and three children, three of Mr. Cornell's youngest daughters, and many others in both families, amounting in the whole to 28 souls, and escaped out of Mr. Cornell's back door, with the children on our shoulders, and the*

> *water up to our chins, wading near 250 or 300 yards to the highest ground, in order to preserve our lives, which under the provident care of Almighty God was most fortunately effected."*

Smith lost more than his house: "My wharfs, warehouse, its contents of corn, salt, sugar &c my dry good store totally gone, with about 800 l. sterling of goods in it; my books, bonds, notes, papers, paper money, specie (some part of which I found again) together with several other houses, and their contents of considerable value."

Cornell came out no better; his "ready Money store kept by Partridge at the Corner opposite Mr. Ellis's destroyed with all the Goods and Money, and the Store Keeper so bruised that it is thought he cannot live." Smith added to Cornell's losses his brig, wharf and warehouses.

James Davis, the colony's printer and publisher of a weekly newspaper, saw his business wash away, shutting down his paper for a year. "Mr. Davis's House [is] a mere Wreck," Howe would write the governor. "His printing Office [is] broke to Pieces, his Papers destroyed and Types buried in the Sands." Davis and his children would spend some of the coming days combing the shore for those types, and some would show up later, possibly found by someone else to be used in the making of counterfeit bills.

"Sixty odd houses are totally destroyed," Smith wrote, "and a large number of others much damaged."

"Newbern is really now a Spectacle," Howe observed. "Her Streets full of the Tops of Houses, Timber, Shingles, Dry Goods, Barrels & Hogsheads, empty most of them, Rubbish &c &c: in so much that You can hardly pass along."

Considering the descriptions, it is amazing how few lives were lost. "Five white people and two black people are drowned," Smith declared, with "many others bruised in the ruins of fallen houses."

Of course the damage spread well beyond New Bern. Williamsburg ran a long list of ships broken up or run aground while Smith quoted a sailing captain who described passing several ships damaged and adrift at sea.

Tryon, who would indeed blame the hurricane on his celestial visitor, recognized that a bigger disaster would result from the storm. "It is imagined that as the Corn was within six Weeks of its Maturity, the Planters may save about half a Crop, but they have no hopes of recovering the Rice lying at this period under Water from the freshes that this Gust occasioned.

"The Country will I fear be greatly distressed this Winter for Provisions as far as this Gale has extended, for the People will not only be short of Corn, but the Hogs which are the support of many Families will lose the Acorns and Nuts in the Woods which used to fat them for Market."

The visitations of Hurricane Floyd and others in recent years helps us remember that the past is sometimes almost closer than the present. "A few days ago so flourishing and thriving," as Mr. Howe concluded, "it shows the Instability of all Sublinary Things."

Miss Margaret Tryon: The Tragic Life of the Governor's Daughter

Margaret Tryon was a three-year-old toddler skipping about the deck when she crossed the ocean with her father William Tryon, the new governor of North Carolina in 1764; and she was just nine when her family arrived for a one-year residence in the palatial, controversial governor's palace in New Bern in June 1770.

Her brief life in our town reflected her brief life in this world, for she would die at age thirty, while carrying a romantic liaison to a tragic end.

Our sources give us hints rather than facts about her life, but the little that we know is interesting and colorful. In a chatty note to his uncle Sewallis Shirley in 1765, for instance, the governor-to-be gave some clue of his fondness for her when he described their first American home: "There is a piaza Runs Round the House both Stories of ten feet Wide with a Ballustrade of four feet high, which is a great Security for my little girl." In the same letter the governor, whose constitution left him frequently ill, sounded almost envious as he wrote, "As to Health Mrs. Tryon and the little girl have enjoyed a happy share of it. As to myself I cannot say so much…"

Hers was a life of regimen, possibly to be expected since her father was a military man and her mother the daughter of a past governor of Bombay. But to some Colonial Americans it seemed overly strict. Lady Anne Blair, a Williamsburg dame, described a relationship between Margaret and her mother (also named Margaret) as if it were a scene from *Mommy Dearest*: "They have a little Girl with them that is equaly to be pitied, this poor thing is stuck up in a Chair all day long with a Coller on, nor dare she even to taste Tea, fruit Cake, or any little Triffle offer'd her by ye Company." In Mrs. Tryon's defense, I must also point out that Lady Anne's other comments on the governor's wife were so catty as to make a reader long to give her milk.

Tryon Palace, the home of Miss Margaret Tryon from 1770–1771. *Photo by the author.*

Her room in New Bern was spacious (its facsimile is on view today at Tryon Palace), her family was active in church and she doubtless played with the children of the city's leading men, though her closest playmate may have been her governess, Ann Patterson.

In June 1771, ten-year-old Margaret and her family sailed for the governor's mansion at Fort George, New York. There, a late-night fire nearly took her life in December 1773.

William Smith, a councilman and friend of the governor, witnessed the conflagration. "I fell in with the Govr. & patrolled with him," he would write. "Thro' the whole he maintained a serene & firm Spirit, except when he told me of his Daughters Situation at the first Discovery."

The governor and his wife had escaped, but Margaret was still in her room, three floors up. Tryon offered a hundred guineas to a man who tried to rescue her but was driven back by the flames.

Happily, Ann Patterson, who slept in her mistress's room, kept a level head. Waking to the alarm, she grabbed the girl and carried her down a smoke-filled stairway. They came out in the second-floor dining room where, strangely enough, Ann left Margaret scurrying back and forth in terror while the governess dashed off in an attempt to rescue Mrs. Tryon's jewels from her dressing room. But the governor's cries for his daughter, floating to her ears from outside, brought her back to her senses. Scooping Margaret up, Ann threw her out a window, where snow and a crowd of waiting people broke her fall.

Revolution put an end to Mr. Tryon's American career. Back in England, Margaret found a post as maid of honor to Queen Charlotte, with whom she often attended plays at Drury Lane. Margaret must have loved the atmosphere of the theater, for she counted a young actress named Miss Woolery among her friends.

Margaret was also an acquaintance of the famous diarist and novelist Fanny Burney, whose journal gives a brief glimpse of young Lady Margaret's chatty personality:

> *All I shall mention of this town visit is, that, the day after the great Drawing-room, Miss Fuzilier, for the first time since I have been in office, called upon me to inquire after the queen. Miss Tryon, and Mrs. Tracey, and Mrs. Fielding were with her. She looked serious, sensible, interesting. I thought instantly of the report concerning Mr. Fairly, and of his disavowal: but it was singular that the only time she opened her mouth to speak was to name him! Miss Tryon, who chatted incessantly, had spoken of the great confusion at the Drawing-room, from the crowd: "It was intended to be better regulated."*

She died in July 1791. Margaret's father had died three years before. Though she was now thirty, Margaret was still very much under her mother's control. Perhaps Mrs. Tryon had begun playing matchmaker, arranging a socially suitable marriage for her daughter. If so, Margaret, like a young heroine in the comedies she loved to see, had her eye on someone further from her "society" but closer to her heart. She chose to elope with a young officer in the Life Guards—the same regiment her father had once commanded.

On the night of the elopement, a rope ladder was dropped from her window. As her beau watched from below, she climbed out, placed her foot on the ladder's rung—and slipped. The young man watched in horror as his intended fell and impaled herself on the palisade fence. We don't know if she lingered or died instantly, but the family vault states that on July 28, 1791, she passed away.

Touring Tryon Palace today and looking upon the typical toys that decorate this little girl's room, I think of the innocence presented and the tragedy coming just down the road. It gives me pause because I have two little girls of my own.

Part II

Revolutionary New Bern

Photograph by Karen Mason.

Mr. Cogdell and His Lovely Daughters

A judge and former sheriff who had tangled with Spanish pirates, Mr. Cogdell must have been the bane of every young man in New Bern—for he stood between them and his several beautiful daughters.

Samuel Cogdell, (1724–1787) traced his roots to the original 1710 settlement of Baron de Graffenried in New Bern: the original family name was Coxdaile, and they were among the "upper class" Swiss.

Born and raised in Beaufort, North Carolina, he was an ensign with the Carteret militia when it beat off an attack of Spanish pirates in 1747. His courage in that tussle must have been noted, for in 1748 he was named sheriff.

Apparently sheriffdom did not appeal to him, for that same year he moved to Johnston County where he opened a mercantile business. In 1752 he met a Massachusetts girl named Lydia Duncan, liked her and married her. He was twenty-six and she, twenty-two. This Tarheel lovebird and his Yankee wife would make ten children, six growing to adulthood. Five of those were girls: Anne (the oldest, born 1753), Margaret, Sarah, Susannah and Lydia, the youngest, born in 1765.

Most of them were born in New Bern, for Mr. Cogdell pulled up his Johnston County stakes and drove them into our sandy soil in 1756. He bought a "good house in tenantable repair" of twenty-four by fifteen feet (it would become less tenantable when a 1769 hurricane washed it away). For a few years he ran a tavern—"ordinary" was the quaint term of the day, but it failed or was sold by 1763. He was loyal to his family: he loaned them the money to purchase a plantation and apparently never asked for that money to be repaid. His mother willed the plantation to him in 1772, declaring it "an act of justice."

The Cogdells were regular churchgoers at the Anglican Christ's Church in town. Samuel was a strong supporter of Governor Tryon

One of Mr. Cogdell's daughters, Anne Cogdell Stanly. *Photo by Kyle Arrowood. Courtesy of Tryon Palace Historic Sites and Gardens.*

in 1771, even serving as an officer in the Battle of Alamance, but the winds of independence would stir his soul and he would become an ardent advocate of freedom after 1775. It must have made for some lively conversations between him and his severely loyalist pastor, James Reed, when they shook hands each Sunday at the door.

Mr. Cogdell was a supporter of education (with five children, who wouldn't be?). He sponsored bills for the New Bern Academy and served on the school's controversial board. He was also, like any well-to-do man of his day, a slave owner and occasionally hired out their services. We know at least that he received pay for the rental of several slaves, including a girl or woman named Dina who worked on the Alamance foray.

One source of his income in New Bern was as justice of the peace. As with his family, he was generous to the community and once signed a petition to spare the lives of two young counterfeiters who'd been sentenced to death. Possibly he had sympathized with them as they'd gone through his own court. Governor William Tryon honored the petition and released the youths.

Later, in the young nation, Mr. Cogdell would serve on the Committee of Safety for Craven County, as a postmaster and as one of the first state treasurers. His signature would appear on a number of bills.

But what about those daughters?

The eldest one, Anne, would marry in 1773. And, while her groom would not be any aged Arthur Dobbs waiting to cross the bar and leave her his fortune, she did make a very nice catch in John Wright Stanly. It makes for a most romantic story:

Stanly was a man of considerable wealth and future through privateering in New Bern, though when they met he'd just gotten out of debtor's prison in Philadelphia. Had it not been for Anne, John would have made his name in Charles Town, for that's where he was trying to go.

However, a stormy day forced his ship to come into port at Beaufort. Traveling with him was his friend, New Bern lawyer and coroner John Sitgreaves, who invited him to travel for a short stay in New Bern. Attending a ball that night, he danced with Anne. By the end of the set the beautiful Miss Cogdell had swept all thoughts of Charles Town from his mind: one of New Bern's greatest family legacies was born.

Six years later another Stanly—John's brother Wright—would come to town and join his brother in the art of marrying Cogdells. Susannah became his wife on September 21, 1779.

We read of another of Mr. Cogdell's daughters striking another man's heart with joy in 1787. The daughter who caught the gentleman's eye was very likely his youngest, Lydia, now twenty-six. In his will, written two years prior to this, Mr. Cogdell had left his personal estate for her use after the passing of her mother, "the rest of my children being already provided for and she being the youngest." This suggests that her other sisters were already married.

William Attmore, a man whose journals are on record, wrote about his visit to New Bern in November of 1787: "At Mr. Green's I saw the pretty Miss Cogdell, whom Mr. Green introduced to me—when the Tea Tackle began to rattle, I was sorry I had previously declared an engagement at Smith's—and was therefore obliged to move…"

The next day William attended the races in town, which he rather enjoyed. Then he dined with Mr. Green again, and we suspect he enjoyed that even more: "There was Miss Cogdell," Attmore wrote. Could Mr. Green have been playing matchmaker? Though an entertaining thought, it is admittedly a leap of logic, but whole species of man have been proposed and accepted on smaller bits of teeth and bone.

If Mr. Green *was* playing yente, it was for naught, for Lydia would walk the aisle with a fellow named Thomas Badger six years later on June 6, 1793. This Mr. Badger was quite a catch as well: he would become a superior court judge, secretary of the navy and a U.S. senator.

And so we have it: one story of love at first sight, another of love unrequited. As demonstrated by the Cogdell women, sometimes life is just a Nicholas Sparks novel.

Alexander Gaston: Patriot with a Medicine Bag

He was a Patriot who would father a judge, tend the American wounded, battle with a printer (and possibly his cow) and in the end die for the cause of freedom.

Born in 1735, Alexander Gaston's ancestors were Huguenots none too fond of persecution, who had left France for Ireland's shores in the seventeenth century. He grew up among shamrocks and leprechaun tales, developing an interest in both medicine and the sea. After training at Glasgow University, he took up his trepanning saws, signed onto His Majesty's Navy and left Ireland forever.

In 1762 the young doctor watched from on deck as his fleet relieved Spain of Cuba. However, the sailors were visited with a major run of dysentery (I wish I could say "pun unintended"), and the good doctor himself suffered a serious bout of the runs. He was so ill by 1764 that he resigned his military post and settled in New Bern to better his health. He purchased two thousand acres of land near the Trent River, a couple of miles from town and bought a townhouse as well.

Dr. Gaston quickly made a name for himself as doctor and apothecary; it was not long before he was a leading citizen.

His name crops up first as a signer of a petition for the hiring of a schoolmaster in 1765: a civic-minded exercise since he would not marry for another eleven years. Occasionally the *Colonial Records* cite his treating militiamen for wounds. We also have an advertisement of his, published in James Davis's *Gazette* in 1778, in which he offers to sell his overstock of drugs. This item gives us a peek at an eighteenth-century doctor's bag of goods: "I have just opened a large assortment of fresh imported medicines…and…would be able to supply others, at the lowest terms with what ever they may want, of Peruvian bark, camphire, a sweet mercury, opium, rheubarb, jalap, Ipecacuanha, aloes, myrrh, gummastick, magnesia, Spanish flies, Venice treacle, borax, saltpeter, volatile salt of harstshorn, do. of salamoniac, camomile flower, brimstone, and flowers of sulphur, &c &c."

I'm very curious about those Spanish flies.

Dr. Gaston's Huguenot ancestors doubtless got friction burns from spinning in their graves when he took on a Catholic bride in May of 1775. Margaret Sharpe, a Cumberland County, England, girl was in town visiting her brothers when Dr. Gaston wooed her.

The Gastons would both become fans of the revolution. It was he, along with fellow patriots Abner Nash and Richard Cogdell, who followed up Royal Governor Martin's flight from town by seizing six pieces of artillery and turning them over to the Patriot cause. Dr. Gaston was named to New Bern's Committee of Safety, a kind of watchdog group aimed at keeping Tories and potentially rebellious slaves in line—the latter purpose due to rumors that Martin aimed to stir them up against their masters. Over the next few years, Dr. Gaston was regularly in touch with Governor Caswell, keeping up a steady discourse regarding troop movements and other issues of war.

Tories, in particular, did not like Gaston. Nor did the Patriot James Davis, who took him to court over the death of his bull in May 1778. (The cause of death—whether by gun, carriage or if the animal was alleged to have died as a result of poor doctoring—we are not told). Davis had a particular dislike of Dr. Gaston, whom he considered to be French. Of course, Gaston was really Irish, although he did have French ancestry and his wife had been raised in a Calais convent. Within days of the bovine slaying, Davis created a major stir in town that was later determined to be an effort aimed at embarrassing the alleged bull-killing doctor.

The catalyst was a Frenchman named Monsieur Chariol de Placer, who was in town recruiting to raise a regiment of Frenchmen for the American cause. Among the new recruits was a young sailor named Julian Laborcet who, Davis insisted, was one of his son's indentured servants. He took out a warrant to get the man back, but the French sergeant at the barracks refused to honor it. Davis drew up a mob armed with clubs, guns and a "screwed Bayonet," according to a complaint Dr. Gaston would later file. Declaring that "the liberty we

Actors reenact the death of Alexander Gaston at a Ghost Walk event in Cedar Grove Cemetery, New Bern. *Photo by the Karen Mason.*

have been fighting for is about to be taken from us by the damned French," Davis vowed to put every Frenchman to death or run them out of town the next night—and included Dr. Gaston as one of his targets.

The next night, Davis's son led a group of sailors to the barracks. They attacked and beat the recruits and, not knowing what else to do, the town's justices of the peace ordered Laborcet jailed until the legitimacy of Davis's charge could be decided. In the end, Laborcet was set free. In June, Dr. Gaston was found innocent of bovine butchery as well.

Whatever Mr. Davis may have thought about him, Dr. Gaston would prove himself to be a great patriot to the end, as would be proven by the most famous and final event of his life three years later, in the late summer of 1781. But let us study that event through the life of his excellent wife…

Margaret Gaston: The Virtuous Wife

Margaret Gaston was one of those quiet heroes. She was an intense, dedicated and fiercely loyal woman who would risk her life for her husband and raise her son to be a state supreme court judge.

She was born Margaret Sharpe in Cumberland County, England, to a Catholic family around 1755. There was no direct law against being Catholic at that time, but "papists" were often saddled with extra taxes and the ineligibility to serve political office. Like many Catholics of her day, she was sent to France for her education, and it was there, in a convent, where she grew up.

Out of school, Margaret sailed for New Bern to visit her brothers who were doing business there. The reportedly beautiful Margaret met Alexander Gaston, a British naval doctor who had settled in New Bern because of his health. He was a Protestant, of Huguenot ancestry. In an age when tolerance was far too rare, their hearts tangled instead of their doctrines. In 1775 they married.

Her new life was mixed with joy and sorrow: joy with her dearly loved husband and the birth of three children, sorrow from the death of her eldest son and of her two brothers.

Worse was on the way: Margaret's Patriot husband had made of himself a particular stench to the local Tories, who sought an opportunity to capture him. The town of New Bern may have been the capital of North Carolina, but it was undermanned and difficult to defend. Sooner or later the enemy would arrive.

On August 20, 1781, the Gastons and their children, three-year-old William (named after his grandfather) and infant Jane, were at their New Bern home (they also owned a plantation across the river and eight miles off) when word came that the meager American forces protecting the town had been brushed aside by a surprise force of British. Tories were at that moment entering the town, and in their hands Gaston's fate would be uncertain at best.

Though his family was safe enough, Gaston knew that he had better flee. He hurried to the city's wharfs where he procured a scow to be ferried across—but it was too late. One Captain Cox arrived with a band of Tories even as Alexander was pushing off. At that moment Margaret appeared, Jane in her arms. Terrified, she threw herself on her knees between the Tories and her husband, begging for his life. Captain Cox merely called for a musket and, aiming it over the woman's shoulder, shot Gaston dead.

Margaret never got over the event. She refused to leave the body until its burial, fearing the Tories would abuse it, and for the rest of her life she dressed in mourning. She marked each anniversary of his death with fasting and prayer.

Though her heart was broken, her spirit was not. In her husband's absence she fiercely embraced her Catholic faith and determined that she would focus on her young son, teaching him its tenets and developing him into a man of morals and honor. Despite her limited income, Margaret saw to it that young William received a good education. He would pursue law and ultimately become a state supreme court justice who would be noted for his attention to the rights of minorities, both Catholics and African Americans. At thirteen, she would send him to Georgetown, where he would literally become the first student enrolled at that Catholic college. Though ill health would bring him home, he continued his studies first through the New Bern Academy and then through Princeton, where he would graduate.

Her troubles were not over: while her son was in Princeton (he was first in his class), Margaret's home caught fire and burned down. William wanted to come home and work to support her but she refused. "Your education is too near my heart to take you away before you finish your studies," she wrote him. "When you finish your studies I mean to sell as much of my stock as will pay my debts." Hers was a "money doesn't buy happiness" mentality: "If Almighty God be pleased to bless us with good health," she wrote in the same letter, "we have every reason to be thankful and happy…I am happy, and hope to be much more so, when I embrace my beloved William."

Margaret would plan and oversee the construction of a new home—smaller but quite livable—that her Jane would describe to her brother in a letter. "It fronts North and South," she would write, "the West end being twenty feet from that fence where the cedar tree and fig bushes are in the bottom of the garden…The house will be small as to what the other was, being 36 feet by 18 and a piazza to the southwards. Mama purposes leasing the front of the lot, when opportunity offers, till you are of age…She says that you must not laugh at her for putting her house in the garden."

However small the new house would be, William assured his sister, it would be "the most valuable in the world, since it contains two infinitely precious treasurers—the tenderest of mothers and most amiable of sisters."

Judge Henry G. Connor, at the 1914 unveiling of a bust of William Gaston at the House of Representatives in Raleigh, credited Margaret with being the woman behind the success of her son: "In a study of the life of William Gaston, must be placed, in preeminent position, the high qualities, singular devotion of his mother and her influence upon his life."

Added another judge, Mathias E. Manly, "with heroic courage, she met and discharged the trust imposed upon her in a manner which marks her as a woman of singular power of mind and strength of character."

Even King Lemuel's words on "the virtuous wife" couldn't have said it much better.

James Davis: The Good, the Bad and the Printer

I don't mean to abuse any New Bern icons, but it is just possible that James Davis was a strange case of Printer Jekyll and Mr. Hyde.

First, you have to admire the guy.

First printing press. *First* newspaper. He was a civic leader, a patriot, a planter, a businessman; he represented the people as sheriff and assemblyman. He was the guy who printed the colony's money, who lost his house and part of his business in a major hurricane (we can all use a little sympathy) and who served as a warden for his church.

But he was also a man who was litigious, ill-tempered and prejudiced, and who just *might* have been a counterfeiter.

James Davis was a Virginian who appeared in New Bern in 1749 at the age of twenty-eight, bringing with him the only printing press in all the 53,000 square miles of North Carolina. Setting up his house and shop near the present-day city hall, he was turning out the *North Carolina Gazette* by 1751. He further earned his keep with private publishing and, most lucrative of all, by becoming the colony's official printer.

This work included legal documents, assembly records and law codes—not to mention the colony's money.

Davis no doubt endeared himself to New Bernians with his front line fighting to establish the city as the colony's capital. His editorials on the matter are quite entertaining: take, for example, this less-than-loving description of rival capital Wilmington published in August 1764: "Cape-Fear, a place within Fifty Miles of the South Boundary of a Province almost 300 miles wide, and the Passage to it gloomy and dismal, through hot parching Sands, enliven'd now and then with a few Wire-Grass Ridges, and Ponds of stagnant Water…"

Marker showing the location of James Davis's press, next door to the current City Hall, New Bern. *Photo by the author.*

One must wonder, though, about his darker side, hinted at in a number of documents from the *Colonial Records*, the correspondence of William Tryon and the written confession of a condemned man.

We know he was not always popular. In 1754 Davis won a seat in the General Assembly. Petitioners contested his victory and the assembly, reviewing the evidence, ordered up a new election.

He would lead a life of litigation. He caused an uproar in 1772 when he took the highly popular Richard Cogdell, commodities inspector for New Bern, to court for dereliction of duty. A divided court exonerated Cogdell and Mr. Davis reacted by unsuccessfully demanding Cogdell be impeached. In 1778 he would take his fellow patriot, Alexander Gaston, to court on charges of killing his favorite bull (again, the court would rule against Davis), and followed this up by leading a riot against Frenchmen in town as a means of embarrassing his opponent, who was of French ancestry.

The darkest charge against Davis's character is that of counterfeiting.

This crime was a major curse in colonial America: remarkably easy to pull off, it was committed by anyone from doctors to blacksmiths to housewives. In one instance in 1752, counterfeiters were caught forging Pieces of eight and other coins in a swamp near New Bern; the men were hanged.

The penalty was usually death, although those convicted sometimes got their ears or noses cropped instead, as an act of mercy (too bad if they wore spectacles!). Still, it takes capital to make imitation capital: so much counterfeit money was circulating around North Carolina that by December of 1770, Governor Tryon was suspecting that some pretty well-placed and wealthy people had to be involved. "The circulation of so large a quantity of Counterfeited currency among us affords a presumption that persons of more considerable property… have been concerned," he told his assembly.

Was his counterfeiter sitting in the assembly hall, listening as he spoke?

When the hurricane of 1769 destroyed much of Davis's house, he stated that many of the "flowers" and types with which he printed money were washed away. Davis reportedly spent time with his family and the children of the town, combing the river bank for the missing types; his assistant, Robert Hall, would later say that Davis suspected some children kept the types they found.

This £3 note was printed in 1754 by James Davis. *Courtesy Tryon Palace Historic Sites and Gardens.*

Whether in the hands of children, dishonest men or the Naiads of the Neuse, those missing types were a key issue in a court of inquiry regarding counterfeiting, held in August 1770. Hall, James Mansfield (another of Davis's men), and James Davis Jr. were grilled over several days. Suspicion that the storm may simply have been an excuse for the type's disappearance was revealed by the following question: "Do you believe the Types and Flowers were lost or secreted?"

"Lost," Hall insisted.

But the question didn't die; it came up repeatedly through the days of the hearing. One gets the feeling that the court believed there was too much serendipity in the whole affair.

It didn't help that both Hall and Mansfield had a history of counterfeiting: they'd been sentenced to death for the crime in this same town in 1768 and were only spared after thirty-two men signed a petition pleading for clemency.

Nowhere in the records of the hearing is Davis himself questioned or accused; perhaps he was not suspected. However, one does wonder why he was employing convicted counterfeiters to print legitimate bills.

All this is highly circumstantial; Matlock would tear it apart in a courtroom. But we do have one more interesting event to look upon: the execution of Spencer Dew in Duplin, North Carolina, on August 2, 1773.

Dew had been caught helping himself to other people's horses. At the gallows he signed a confession he'd given to the sheriff that was later printed in the Cape Fear *Mercury*. He spoke of counterfeiting operations as much as theft: "I was in combination with James Davis, Printer in New Bern," he said, "and received him Three Hundred Pounds Proc[lamation money]. Which I saw him make to Pass, and I was to give him one half of what I got for it; and in 1773, he also gave me Eight Hundred Pounds of his own make on the same terms." He added that he had seen Davis pass as much as £2,000 in counterfeit bills to an individual, and spoke of another £150 given to a William Stringer "on the same terms that I had mine."

Ending his statement, he went on to test its veracity before the Eternal Judge. Davis was never officially charged; one can question whether the words of a thief and admitted passer of fraudulent bills can be trusted. Could he have borne a grudge?

Even so, a powerful man can always manipulate the courts in his favor. And the last confession of a man in the shadow of the gallows cannot be too easily dismissed.

The verdict is unsure, but we can sympathize with historian Alan D. Watson when, speaking of the governor's conviction of crime in high places, that "Governor Tryon apparently had not been far wrong."

James Reed: Missionary with a Cause

As the first official rector of Christ's Church he was, technically, a missionary. The colonies were, after all, a mission field; North Carolina was little more than a hinterland full of dissenting Methodists, Presbyterians and Quakers when he arrived in 1753, sent along by the Society for the Propagation of the Gospel (SPG), the Church of England's missionary arm.

Even John Lapierre, the old minister he was replacing at the Christ Church parish, was really a Huguenot. Reed had a fervent drive to perform his duty—he would need to. The parish, though founded in 1715, was just now getting around to finishing its first church building, at the corner of Pollock and Middle Streets. Along with this church, he would have to travel extensively, overseeing services, weddings and other ministerial duties at eight chapels in Craven County, as well as serving as chaplain for the general assembly.

Ministers in Reverend Reed's day were sorely underpaid, although Governor Dobbs saw to it that he at least received some additional remuneration from the SPG. Settling down to domestic bliss by marriage to a local widow, Hannah Stringer, James hunkered down for the long haul, laying "aside all thoughts of deserting my Charge or ever moving."

He would stay until his death in 1777, surviving three colonial administrations and the early stages of a revolution that he strongly opposed.

James kept a steady stream of correspondence with the secretary of the SPG, often discussing church and educational matters, his health and gossip of other missionaries in the colony.

In August 1765 he suffered a serious bout of yellow fever: "The attack was exceeding violent, but soon over as is common in that disorder and

The steeple of the "new" Christ's Church (1800s) rises over the trees of the churchyard. *Photo by the author.*

left me exceeding deaf," he wrote the following January. "Since [that time] I have enjoyed as good a state of health as ever I did since I came into America my hearing excepted which gives me great uneasiness."

Along with his own illnesses, he saw to the health of his brethren. Alexander Stewart, who was the rector at St. Thomas Parish in Bath, for instance, arrived in New Bern quite sick at the end of 1765. "Mr. Stewart was brought here in an Horse litter about a month ago and has been ever since under the care of the Doctor—This afflicted Brother has lost the use of his limbs with the Rheumatism and can hardly support his own weight with the assistance of a pair of Crutches."

Another letter gives some indication of his typical schedule: "I have made two excursions very lately into remote Parishes, preached for several days together and until I grew hoarse and baptized upwards of two hundred Children and Adults—such journeys are very disagreeable for Churches or Chapels or tolerable accommodations are rarely to be met with—I have likewise visited Saint Johns Parish which is a very small one and contiguous to Craven County four different times during these last six months and baptized Thirty five White Children and one Black and administered the sacrament of the Lords Supper to Thirty nine Communicants at Newport Chapel…"

James was popular with both governors and his congregations. Leading men in the town often assisted, reading sermons when he was absent and helping to raise money for the church and the school.

A public school was his biggest dream and perhaps his finest accomplishment. From its inception in 1764 he struggled through victories and failures to convince the assembly to approve its construction, to raise the money for a building and teacher and finally to keep it running. The New Bern Academy, as it came to be called, would teach both boys and girls; while much of the schoolmaster's salary would come through tuition, the school's trustees set aside funds to pay for up to five poor students' tuition. Reed himself often contributed portions of his own meager salary to the school's development.

Like many ministers, James was a tried-and-true Tory opposed to the Patriot cause. His first big conflict in this area came in July 1775, when the Continental Congress called for "a day of fasting, humiliation and prayer to humble ourselves before God." The main point of the service was to honor Boston Patriots who were suffering under the punishment imposed on them by the King. On July 20, the town's Safety Committee visited with the pastor over coffee, calling on him to perform the service and give a sermon on the subject. Being a representative of the King's church, he refused, asking "for a little liberty as yourself" to "do my duty."

Such liberty as James asked for was not allowed: the committee demanded that the vestry suspend him and tradition claims boys playing drums started meeting him at the church door, protesting his views.

"To live peaceably with all men, if possible, was my determined Resolution, and after the Committee's suspension I lived very retired for two or three months," he later wrote the SPG. His congregation began to miss him and, despite their political differences, invited him back. "About the middle of November [1775] last Providence presented an opportunity of decently closing the breach." He ended this letter with a hope that "the speedy and merciful interposition of the King of Kings may restrain the exorbitant passions of men, check the desolating progress of civil discord, and heal the ghastly wounds of our country."

Other problems of revolution weighed heavily on him, including a shutdown of North Carolina's courts, instituted by her last royal governor, Josiah Martin. One result of this was a collapse of the collecting of taxes to support the ministers of the churches. "I am heartily weary of living in this land of perpetual strife and contention," he wrote the Secretary.

Other problems continued to strike the loyalist preacher: in December 1776, the church was officially disestablished from the Church of England, and taxes for its support were eliminated. To keep ministers from dabbling too much in politics, the new state's new Constitution declared clergymen to be ineligible to serve as a member of the House, Senate or state council unless they first resigned their pastoral responsibilities.

Still, he kept his earlier word and hung on to the end. On May 7, 1777, he passed away, living to see the people he loved declare their independence, but not to see their independence fulfilled. His twenty-five years' service is the longest of any rector in Christ's Church's history. His wife survived him, but he left no children. He was, according to Dr. G.W. Paschal, Baptist historian, "A very worthy man and the most influential of the Episcopal ministers who labored in North Carolina before the revolution."

John Wright Stanly: From Prison to Privateer

He was everything you'd want your daughter never to bring home: a chronic gambler, a convicted counterfeiter, a debtor and a jailbird. But John Stanly was able to sweet-talk his way into the heart of the daughter of Richard Cogdell, one of New Bern's most eminent citizens—and ultimately became more eminent than Cogdell.

He was John Wright Stanly. Born in 1742 and orphaned by 1759, the young ne'er-do-well plied the streets of Williamsburg with such upstarts as fellow redhead Thomas Jefferson, a student in William and Mary College. He loved to gamble—no crime unless you were bad at it, which he was. His debts and unsavory friends convinced him to try his hand at counterfeiting. Apparently none too talented at that, either, he was caught and lodged in a Williamsburg jail. The sentence for counterfeiting was death, though if your judge was unusually lenient, he might just order your ears cut off. Somehow, Stanly escaped both.

He moved to Jamaica where he gambled and grew poor. He was beginning to show some business acumen, however, and signed up as a partner with a merchant named Jonathan Cowpland. For a while they worked together, transporting cargo from Kingston to Philadelphia. Cowpland, apparently unscrupulous in his pursuit of wealth, discovered Stanly's past and used it to escape the partnership by accusing him of falsifying records. He declared to all that Stanly had saved his own neck by turning evidence and sending five men to the gallows (no evidence for this exists) and saddled him with a huge debt which the business had previously accrued.

Stanly tried desperately to pay off the wrongful debt, but was arrested and shipped to a Philadelphia debtor's prison before it could be done. There he spent the next couple of years, dealing with his creditors and hiring lawyers to straighten out the whole mess. To gain

The John Wright Stanly House, currently part of Tryon Palace Historic Sites and Gardens. *Photo by the author.*

favor in a town where he was unknown and Cowpland was respected, he wrote a series of pamphlets presenting his case. Eventually he gained both popularity and freedom, along with a handsome financial settlement from his foe.

Though vindicated, he'd had enough of the City of Brotherly Love. He set his eyes on Charles Town, South Carolina.

Fate and a beautiful woman got in his way.

While visiting New Bern en route, he met Anne Cogdell at a ball. They fell in love and married on June 24, 1773. Now New Bernian, he struggled for a few years to make ends meet in a world hobbled by England's punitive trade laws. For Stanly, the Revolution was almost a godsend for business, for the Continental Congress, lacking any real navy, called anxiously for privateers.

Privateering: it was legalized piracy or a gentleman's navy, depending on whether it supplied you or boarded you. The business was dangerous—especially when you were matching yourself against the most powerful navy in the history of the world. A privateer had to buy his ship, its munitions and supplies before playing games of cat and mouse with enemy ships-of-the-line. Darting into and out of guarded ports, these gentlemen rapscallions stalked mercantile and smaller military ships under the British flag, then raced home with any booty they bagged.

More often then not, they didn't get there. They were run aground, captured in distant bays or seized on the sea by the ever-vigilant Brits. The odds were calculated as high as six-to-one against a privateering ship's safe return. But those who made it brought large enough profits to make their owners very rich men.

Despite the risks, it was a tempting venture for all involved. Every man earned a cut of the profits, his share depending on his role in the crew. Even a cabin boy could end a cruise well off if his ship did well. Besides, discipline was not so tight on a privateer as in the navy; a sailor was much less likely to become intimate with the punishing lash.

Stanly became rich but not through avarice—he once loaned a huge sum of money to General Nathaniel Greene to keep the Continental Army afloat, and was said to have bailed out his old nemesis Cowpland at one time. Working from his home in New Bern until 1781 when his city was overrun and he moved to Philadelphia, he sent out his fleet of ships, including one he named the *Sally*, a pet name for Anne. Some ships he named for fellow patriots, such as the *Caswell* and the *General Nash*. Among his most successful privateers were the *Nancy* and the interestingly named *The Sturdy Beggar*. Most of these ships were two-masted schooners, usually armed with a dozen or so heavy guns.

In one incident his fourteen-gun *Nancy* captured a ten-gun British sloop, the *Severn*, near Jamaica. While escorting the *Severn* home the *Nancy* was in turn captured by a twenty-gun ship. Two days later, a Continental craft captured the British ship in turn and set the *Nancy* free. War is a fickle thing.

Peacetime trade was more difficult for Stanly, but he did reasonably well, making molasses at a distillery, which he'd purchased after it had been confiscated from loyalist Samuel Cornell.

The Stanlys raised several children at their elaborate home, including the troublesome but charismatic John Stanly Jr. John Wright is also generally believed to be the father of John Caruthers Stanly, a wealthy black man sired through the slave of the captain of one of Stanly's vessels.

John and his wife, Anne, would both die in the prime of life, victims of a yellow fever epidemic, which could make coastal towns a death trap in the hot, humid summers. John died on June 1, 1789, and Anne would follow just one month later on July 2. They left behind several dependent children, including their youngest, Margaret, only two years old.

The John Wright Stanly House: George Washington Slept Here

Yeah, yeah, I know: George Washington slept *everywhere*. There's probably an oyster bar in Boise that says he did. But he really *did* sleep in New Bern. And danced here, too, at the Tryon Palace, which was "hastening to ruins." Those are his words, straight from the icon's mouth.

George Washington most likely slept in the John Wright Stanly House in 1791, when he was swinging through New Bern as part of his southern tour. Unlike the hastening ruins at which he danced, his night's accommodations were "exceeding good." The Stanlys had vacated the house two years earlier, being incommoded by death; their orphaned children were not yet of an age to take the place over.

It is a curious edifice. As John Wright Stanly watched the building go up, he probably had no premonition as to the schizophrenic life it would lead over the next 225 years. It would not only sleep a president; it would also birth or house governors, a friendly general, an enemy general and, by reputation, at least a couple of ghosts. It would serve as a convent and a library as well as be uprooted and moved twice.

That's pretty lively for a two-story pile of dry wood and plaster.

Stanly House first went up in 1783 at the corner of Middle and New Streets, built with privateering profits from the Revolutionary War. In fineness, it was second only to Tryon Palace, which was still a few years from its fiery fate. Mr. Stanly had hired John Hawks, the English architect who had designed and constructed the Palace itself, to design his home.

This Georgian residence features wooden quoins at its corners and a hip roof with a railing. The interior has a fine stairway and transverse arch, Greek moldings and pedestal mantels. Now, some people can study a house and lecture for hours on its finer points, but I am one of these guys who pretty much looks around and—borrowing

The John Wright Stanly House makes its final crosstown move. *Courtesy Tryon Palace Historic Sites and Gardens.*

my daughter's phrase—says, "Wow. Cool as mess." I don't have a clue what "cool as mess" means, but to be honest, I'm not sure what a quoin or a hip roof is, either. So, if you would like a detailed report of its architecture, I recommend taking the tour at Tryon Palace Historic Sites and Gardens.

When John Jr., the dueling son of John Wright Stanly, came of age, he moved back home. One of his daughters, Elizabeth, would marry a War of 1812 hero named Walker Keith Armistead (Stanly would *not* be happy). While visiting her parents in 1817, she livened things up by going into labor and delivering one of New Bern's more famous sons, General Lewis A. Armistead, who would march to a glorious death at Gettysburg.

In 1828 John Stanly Jr.'s son Alfred would receive control of the house, then sell it in turn to his brother Alexander. In 1834, it would sell out of the family to George Pollock.

During the Civil War the Stanly House served both God and Country.

When the occupying Union army arrived on March 14, 1862, General Ambrose Burnside was quick to select it as his headquarters. General Armistead must have winced when he heard the news.

By the end of October, however, Country gave way to God and a convent of nuns called the Sisters of Mercy moved in.

These ladies had sailed from New York to work in the Union hospitals. Susan Messenger, a kind of camp follower to the Forty-fifth Massachusetts, described how the house was transformed:

> [Governor Stanly] *hardly expected a convent bell would ever be hung on his elegant staircase. One parlor was left furnished to receive the world's people; the other was their chapel, furnished with altar, etc. All the rest of the rooms were simply furnished, iron bedsteads, one chair in each and a wash-stand, save one room, in which Washington had slept when in New Berne, and which was also General Burnside's apartment; this house having been first his Headquarters. This room was kept for the "recreation-room" for the sisters. A table in the centre, a desk and books, a few chairs, no carpet, no feminine look, save the exquisite neatness which pervaded the whole house.*

In 1884, the house—which had cost $20,000 to build—sold for $7,100 to James Bryan, a former Confederate major. Interestingly, his wife was from the Spaight family, avowed enemies of John Jr. It was about this time that neighbors first reported ghosts floating about the place—supposedly former Stanlys stirred up by the presence of Spaights.

The house was moved to another location on New Street in 1935 to make way for a new post office. There, it was sold to the New Bern Library Association—this time for $6,000. It maintained its humble and bookish existence until 1966, when the library's directors offered it to the Tryon Palace Commission as a free gift, so long as the Commission agreed to restore it and display it to the public. The TPC prepared to move the edifice one last time.

Notice how this house started out at $20,000, then sold cheaper and cheaper until it was finally turned over for free. If the trend keeps up, the Palace Commission will eventually feel obliged to pay someone $5,000 to take it. Perhaps I should apply.

If left to itself, a potato will sprout eyes. The same goes for old houses and additions. Like a worthy chef, restorers carved out those "eyes" and hauled the house once more to its present George Street location. It was opened to the public in 1972.

Today, you will find no praying nuns clanging their bell; no wakes are in progress for victims of Yellow Jack; no slumbering snore of a man with wooden teeth; no toasts to the Yankee capture of a town nor a whispered reminder, "That book is late. Twenty-five cents, please." Instead of the chatter of children, you'll hear the dialogue of a docent: "Its gracious center hall plan and grand two-story stairwell are as striking today as they were for eighteenth-century visitors," she'll say. And you will respond, "Wow. Cool as mess."

George Washington: Dancing and Dinner on the Southern Tour

He was going to visit the whole country, he told Edward Rutledge in January 1791, so long as his health and circumstances would permit. When Washington told North Carolinian assemblyman William Blount about his plans, the gentleman was ecstatic. Maybe this would "induce the Overseers of the Roads and Ferry-Keepers to mend *their Ways* and repair or build new Boats," Blount wrote a friend. (He must have been a practical man.)

The President was anxious to begin. He wanted nothing to do with traipsing the coastal rivers and savannahs during the malarial summer months so he decided to leave in the spring. Why die of yellow fever when you can hold off a few years and be put under by a medical quack?

He would leave in March, visiting all the major southern towns: Richmond, Petersburg, New Bern, Wilmington, Georgetown, Charleston and Savannah, after which he would return to Philadelphia by an inland route. It would add spice to his routine, rally the people and help him learn the country he governed.

Much to the delight of local historians he, as always, kept a careful journal on the way.

"Left Philadelphia about 11 O'clock to make a tour though the Southern States," he announced on Monday, March 21. On April 16 he crossed the border into North Carolina. He had a mild reception in Halifax and then reached Tarboro, "less than Hallifax, but more lively and thriving." The folks at Tarboro had little warning he would arrive but, Washington admitted, "We were recd. at this place by as

One of thousands of "George Washington Slept Here" markers in America—and this one is true! *Photo by the author.*

good a salute as could be given with one piece of artillery." This was followed by dinner at a "trifling place" in Greenville.

With acts like this, New Bern certainly had an opportunity to make a grand show.

Washington had started April 20 with a faux pas when his party arrived at what they assumed was a "public house" or tavern run by a Colonel Allen. He did not know it was Allen's personal home: "We were very kindly & well entertained without knowing it was at his expence until it was too late to rectify the mistake," Washington noted that night.

New Bern saw to it that a party—at least three parties, in fact—showed up to escort him. Perhaps it was overkill: he was pleased, it seemed, by "a small party of Horse" led by Judge Sitgreave, who met him at Street's Ferry ten miles above New Bern (he spelled it "Newburn"). However, you can almost hear him groan when he added, "another small party of horse under one Simpson, met us at Greensville, and in spite of every endeavor which could comport with decent civility, to excuse myself from it, they would attend me to Newburn."

At the edge of town he was joined by the New Bern Volunteer Infantry, which by this point must have made for quite a parade. He reached his lodgings where Captain Stephen Tinker's artillery company fired him a fifteen-gun salute. The infantry, not to be outdone, fired off fifteen volleys, while the houses were illuminated in his honor. Finally he was allowed to retire to his accommodations, which he described as "exceeding good."

He does not identify this home, but it was most likely the John Stanly House. Washington had stated his intentions of not staying in private homes so as to not be a burden, and the Stanly House was vacant at the time. As the finest residence in town, it certainly met the criteria of "exceeding good."

Washington wrote a careful, textbook description of New Bern that night: "This town is situated at the confluence of the rivers Nuse & Trent, and though low is pleasant…It stands on a good deal of ground, but the buildings are sparce and altogether of Wood; some of which are large & look well. The number of Souls are about 2000. Its exports consist of Corn, Tobacco, Pork—but principally stores & lumber."

The next day he went to "what they call the Pallace—formerly the government House & a good brick building but now hastening to ruins." Tryon Palace was not yet an old building; it had been completed only twenty years before. But it had not been lived in for some time. The abuse of time and revolution had turned it into a cross between a dancing hall and classrooms, though the assembly still occasionally met there. Even in 1784 a German traveler had described the place as "almost in ruins." William Attmore, a diarist visiting from Philadelphia in 1787, also noted, "The King of G. Britain's Arms, are still suffered to appear in a pediment at the front of the Building which…appears Something strange." Did anyone give those arms a nervous glance as the President walked inside?

If so, Washington didn't give enough thought to mention it. Instead, he spoke of a public dinner in his honor, and "a dancing assembly in the evening." He is careful to mention that "at the latter there were abt. 70 ladies." He must have enjoyed dancing with them very much—with Martha, who was unwilling to tackle the rigors of this trip, at home, there was no one to cast a warning eye!

The next morning, under another escort of horse, gentlemen and yet another round of cannon, Washington and his entourage left for Wilmington. Perhaps the escorts had gotten the hint in Greenville: they left him after only a few miles.

By the end of his southern tour, Washington would travel for three and a half months, covering 1,800 miles. New Bern's share in the event would be some powder, a dinner and a dance over two nights and a day. But the memory would last more than two hundred years.

Part III

Antebellum New Bern

Photo by the author.

Amelia Green: Homespun Freedom

By the standards of her day she was a nobody—a slave who'd managed to purchase her own freedom, in part because she was middle-aged and therefore less valuable as chattel.

Her days of slavery had been lived out at the Schawfield Plantation in Cape Fear, and she bought her way to freedom on May 18, 1785, "advanced in life" (she later described) "with the infirmities of age" upon her. Because, even in the best of circumstances, the status of freedom was always on thin ice, she filed for her freedom both through the local courts and through the state assembly, signing the legal documents with her "mark."

We do not know when she was born—or even when, exactly, she died (it was somewhere between 1820 and 1824). But on the day she became free, four of her five children were still enslaved. Over the coming years she would struggle to help them achieve their emancipation. The court records tell us about that, and it is enough wherefore to remember her.

Those children included a boy and four daughters, with the youngest, Princess Green, only five at the time of her mother's manumission. The other children were Richard Green, her eldest and already an adult, Nancy, Charlotte and Harriet. Freeing them could be a difficult game: not only was there the problem raising the money, but she would also have to convince different masters to let them go. It was typical in Antebellum days that slave families were not kept together, but sold off or given as gifts to children who were marrying or leaving home.

Her son had gained his freedom through his master's good will and respect four years before his mother. The others would not see theirs for more than ten years, however. Amelia's activities during that time are

A character interpreter at Tryon Palace portrays a nineteenth-century slave. *Photo by the author.*

unknown. She lived in the city, spinning to earn her bread and board, saving every penny she could to purchase her daughters' freedom.

The first one freed was Nancy Handy, at a cost of 120 pounds, in 1794. Nancy earned the price of her freedom herself and would later free her own two daughters, Louisa and Betsy. But Amelia was there, guiding her through the complicated legal mazes.

It was all a tricky business: first, a price had to be agreed upon between the master and buyer. The completed transaction was then recorded in the county records. In other southern states that might have finished the business, but North Carolina was unique in that no owner could simply set his slave free. The county courts had to approve their manumission, and proof had to be given that the slaves had shown "meritorious behavior" to earn their freedom and guarantee they would not be a burden on the state. After 1808, a bond even had to be paid upon their freedom. Oftentimes, once a person gained freedom through the county courts, they petitioned the state courts for added insurance.

Even then, a freedman was not without concerns. Not only was there the intense prejudice of the day, but a black man or woman could also be sold into slavery to meet their debts—or, if not careful, could find themselves kidnapped by unscrupulous whites who then sold them back into bondage outside the area. This was the fate of some freedmen in the North, even after those states abolished slavery.

As she scraped and earned, Amelia's heart must have leaped into her throat, for several times her children were sold between various owners. Fortunately for her, they all stayed within the same region, and the families who owned them were interrelated and known to Amelia.

It was only a few months after Nancy's emancipation that Amelia was able to buy Princess Ann, her youngest child, at about sixteen.

Through the years, Amelia steered a cautious course, working with white lawyers and other leaders, earning the respect of the community in which she lived. She made New Bern her home—probably because the town had an unusually large population of about 1,744 free blacks. Also, one of her daughters, Harriet Handy, lived there along with her granddaughter, Peggy. She built a home on land near the site of the old governor's palace, but nearly lost it in 1801 due to tax costs. It was then that her own deeds in freeing her children came back to reward her: Kitty Stanly, her granddaughter (daughter of Princess Ann), was the future wife of John Caruthers Stanly, a free mulatto who was the son of the famous privateer, John Wright Stanly. Though a former slave, John was now one of the wealthiest men in town. He now had slaves of his own, but he did watch out for his own family. He quickly bought up Amelia's lots then granted her a lifetime right to live on them.

In 1805 John purchased Kitty's freedom and married her on March 26.

The home still stands as a private residence, though it has been altered and moved from its original location.

In the midst of her struggles to maintain her home, Amelia continued to work for her children's freedom. Her last child, Harriet, was freed in 1806.

During their lifetimes both Amelia and her relative-by-marriage, John Caruthers Stanly, would free a large number of children, grandchildren and other relatives of Amelia Green. Many African American families today proudly trace their roots to the Greens of New Bern; it was a family that knew how to work together, to survive and excel in difficult times.

Cedar Grove: The Land Beyond the Weeping Gate

We have no Grauman's Chinese Theater, and so New Bern's walk of fame is a cemetery. Rather than admiring handprints in the sidewalk, you can stroll along, your feet crunching on the oyster-shell drive, listening to birds sing from cedars draped in Spanish moss as you read the names of many of our famous sons and daughters, etched in marble and granite stones.

It had started as an Indian cemetery, historian Gertrude S. Carraway suggested—the "hilly part," at least. For some time it was pastureland, located on the edge of town (it is now quite surrounded by town), a nice place to stroll on your way to the horse racetrack.

Prior to 1800, most folks got buried downtown in the Christ's Church grounds. If you go there today you will find a number of the old markers: a few upright and others slabs upon the ground, all weathered, the names sometimes barely legible, their lettering as aged and worn as the bones beneath. James Reed, the colonial parson, lies there; so do the bodies of John and Ann Wright Stanly.

About 1798, a fellow named "Yellow Jack" came to town and, by the time he passed on, New Bern was in pretty desperate need of new graveyard digs.

"Yellow Jack" is yellow fever. Being a wet, coastal town, New Bern was a regular petri dish for the disease. The epidemic of 1798 took a huge toll on the city.

It was a rough couple of years: the Stanlys died of it, one within a month of each other. Scores died in the town and, according to one report, pallbearers in particular were catching the disease and dying rapidly.

Ms. Carraway noted in her book *Crown of Life*, that "So many persons succumbed that at night trenches were dug in the Episcopal

The "Weeping Gate" entrance to the Cedar Grove Cemetery. *Photo by the author.*

church yard in a line…and the bodies were buried indiscriminately." Reverend Thomas P. Irving, a rector of Christ's Church and a schoolmaster at Tryon Palace (the regular school had been burned down by a not-quite-graceful singing class), performed many of the funerals.

In 1800 Irving's church decided new burial space was needed. Cedar Grove was opened to the white population (Greenwood Cemetery would become the burial ground for blacks). One of its earliest residents (buried in 1802) would be Irving's fellow-in-spirit, schoolmaster Thomas Tomlinson, whose grave lies to the left, immediately inside the cemetery's main entrance.

In 1854 the cemetery was turned over to the city, which over time added a number of improvements. That same year a marl wall and three-arch gateway was added. As decorative and attractive as it is, its purpose was primarily aimed at keeping out the cattle, hogs and dogs that were fond of rooting about. The critters found their way in despite the barricade, apparently.

Many of New Bern's most influential residents have made Cedar Grove their final home: State Supreme Court Judge William Gaston,

A ghostly mortician and his wife greet visitors during the Historic Society's annual ghost walk. *Photo by Karen Mason.*

for instance, and his close friend and political ally, John Stanly (Gaston wrote his epitaph). You can find the marker of Caleb Bradham, inventor of Pepsi, or the eighteenth-century painter, William J. Williams (George Washington was among his subjects).

Politicians are as populous here as in Congress itself, inspiring the worms instead of their constituents. Furnifold Simmons and Richard Spaight Donnell are two of the better-known congressional stars.

Confederate generals rest in peace here, as do many of the Confederate casualties of the Battle of New Bern, sleeping together in an underground vault known as the Confederate Memorial.

After passing the unusual gate, the memorial is one of the first things you see: at the end of the main walk, on a circle of a slightly raised mound, an imposing Confederate soldier watches the grounds from his stately pedestal. Beneath his feet lie the dead of battle, their names immortalized on bronze plaques, regiment by regiment.

The memorial got its start as early as 1866 when the Ladies Memorial Association was founded to memorialize their war dead. Raising money through fairs and concerts, the ladies were able to lay a cornerstone for the mausoleum the next year—though the military ordered them to refrain from displaying Confederate flags and banners during the ceremony. The actual memorial was dedicated in 1885.

The Confederate dead of Cedar Grove have been the occasional victims of disrespect: at times their statues have had been found headless, and at least once the mausoleum of dead soldiers was robbed.

Still, Cedar Grove is a pretty place.

So much so, in fact, that Fred Smith, an artist in the Forty-fourth Massachusetts Volunteer Regiment illustrated it during the occupation in 1862.

The cemetery underwent another major facelift in 1883, including the planting of 615 decorative shrubs.

Cedar Grove makes for a fascinating walk, even if you are totally unconcerned with its hoary greats; a camera buff can get lost in here. There is a whole history lesson in the architecture of markers and vaults, from the humble, paper-thin stones of the late 1700s to the marbled spires and statues of the 1800s. Curious "table top" tombs are here: markers in the form of tables on which families actually picnicked in a more mordant age, conversing with the memories of their beloved dead.

Today Cedar Grove is part of the regular trolley tours in town, and every Halloween season it is a favored location of the Historical Society's annual ghost walk, when ghosts of the past haunt about, and a creepy mortician and his wife greet hundreds of visitors with ghoulishly bad humor. They are always sure to remind guests of one of the cemetery's most famous legends—that of the Weeping Gate. "If it weeps on *you*," the mortician says, examining his guests for signs of dripped-upon hair, "You will be the next to visit—feet first!"

The Dueling Stanlys: Politics and Gun Powder

It's hard to believe today, but in the old South men were willing to kill or be killed over an "honor" defined as anything from a political insult or a lady offended to a piece of cake hurled into your cup of tea (I kid you not). Some very great men culled the gene pool in this way, among them Hamilton and Burr (1804) and Andrew Jackson (1813), who would carry a bullet from such a contest in his shoulder for many years.

Duels were usually fought in a more or less remote spot—the woods behind a church, for instance—since they were technically illegal. I read of one duel carried out in a Charleston hotel room ("Be sure you hit your man, gentlemen, the plaster is new."). Those South Carolinians! Go figure.

But New Bern was not immune to dueling. Congressman John Stanly himself killed a man here in 1802: Richard Dobbs Spaight, the state's first native-born governor and a political rival of John.

Neither man was known for his sunny temperament. Spaight was easily riled while Stanly, the son of the privateer John Wright Stanly, was especially adept at goading his foes. "In repartee and sarcasm I never saw his equal," wrote his acquaintance, Stephen Miller. "His efforts in that line were absolutely withering."

Theirs was a spring-summer hate: Spaight was of the Founding Fathers' generation, a relatively old man of forty-four; Stanly was post-revolutionary, just twenty-eight. Stanly was dapper and stylish; Spaight went about in a powdered wig and knickers. At one time both men were Federalists, but President Adams's Alien and Sedition Acts were enough to make Spaight jump parties in 1798.

Character interpreters playing Spaight (the author, left) and Stanly prepare for the worst in a Tryon Palace reenactment of the duel. *Courtesy of Tryon Palace Historic Sites and Gardens.*

Spaight, a Republican congressman since 1798, was unseated by the staunchly Federalist Stanly in 1800. Spaight could not have been happy at the time.

On August 8, 1802, John Stanly was heard deriding Spaight for leaving the Federalist Party; hearing of it, Spaight fired off a challenge to a duel, sending it by way of his friend, Dr. Edward Pasteur. Stanly talked his way out of the spot, but the situation was hardly defused. The two men fired letters back and forth, none of them charitable. Reading them, one is tempted to think they used asbestos-lined paper to keep the notes from catching fire.

Spaight published the letters in the local paper; Stanly replied with a defaming handbill. Spaight turned up the heat with an angrier handbill of his own. Finally, on September 5, Stanly's friend, Attorney Edward Graham, arrived at Spaight's house with a new challenge. At 5:30 p.m. that day they met behind the Masonic Hall. Stanly provided the guns. A large crowd turned out.

In keeping with the popular Code Duello, the men raised their pistols and, standing back to back, paced off. Ordered to "Fire!" they did. Nothing happened, for both men missed.

In many duels, this might have ended it—once a shot was fired, honor was served. Indeed, duels were often more demonstrative than deadly: guns were fired in the air, the deed declared done and everyone went home to sip brandy and remember the day. But neither Stanly nor Spaight would be satisfied with anything but a corpse on the ground. They reloaded and fired again. Stanly's coat collar was clipped.

A third failed round resulted in pleas from the crowd that the contest end. Mr. Graham grabbed Stanly's gun and waved it in the air, offering to shoot the next person who tried to stop the duel.

Finally, a fourth shot found its mark and Richard Dobbs Spaight sunk to the ground. Shot through the side, he was carried off the field. His family watched as he suffered that day and expired the next. His widow would have his untarnished honor to keep her warm at night.

Stanly took to his heels to avoid a murder charge, though later (partly with the help of his close friend, William Gaston) he would receive a governor's pardon. He would live another quarter of a century, spending much of it goading his new political rival, Richard Dobbs Spaight Jr.—his victim's son.

John must have been idolized by his brothers, for three of them would follow in his path.

The most famous of these was that of his brother, Thomas. While attending a party at William Gaston's home about the year 1812, Thomas decided it would be good fun to toss a piece of cake at his friend, Louis D. Henry. The cake landed in a cup of tea which splashed all over Mr. Henry's vest. Now, any teen in the youth group I assist would tell you: a situation like that would be the high point of an after-service meet at Wendy's. However, Mr. Thomas was no member of our youth group. Heated words followed. John, it is said, advised his brother that a duel was just the thing. Thomas agreed: a challenge was issued. Although the earlier Stanly duel had convinced legislators to toughen anti-dueling laws, Mssrs. Stanly and Thomas evaded them by simply stepping over the Virginia border. Mr. Thomas proved to be a dead shot; Mr. Stanly proved to be, more simply, dead.

Later, John's brother Richard tried his dueling hand. His involved swords and was fought in the West Indies. Like Thomas, he wound up dead.

Later, according to Stephen Miller, one more Stanly took a shot at the field of honor when he challenged fellow Congressman Samuel W. Ingle of Alabama. They missed on the first shot, but had enough sense to stop.

"I conclude [the younger Stanlys] were pupils of Harry Hotspur," Miller wryly noted, referring to the Shakespearean brawler. They "needed a counselor less impetuous than their elder brother, whose brow had been encircled by a bloody wreath of honor." As John Stanly's preacher son, Frank, might have said, "Amen to that."

J.C. Stanly: A Peculiarity in the Peculiar Institution

One of the biggest shocks of my overly pampered life was learning that New Bern's biggest slaveholder was an African American. Not only that—he was a former slave. I had another big shock when I learned that he wasn't the only African American in town with slaves: in 1830, thirteen free black families had them, including a bricklayer and plasterer named Donum Mumford.

John Caruthers Stanly—known locally as Barber John—was a mulatto born of an Ebo woman and, it was commonly believed, of John Wright Stanly in 1774. Although his father was one of the most prominent men in town, his mother was a slave. And that meant J.C. was. His masters were Lydia and Alexander Stuart, one of J.W. Stanly's ship captains.

Throughout his life J.C. Stanly would maintain a close relationship with Lydia Stuart, with whom he would walk down the streets and often take to church in her declining years. He would also develop a close relationship with his white stepbrother, the lawyer John Stanly, whom later in life he would bail out of financial trouble—to the ultimate ruin of his own affairs.

But we are getting ahead of ourselves: as a slave, John learned the barbering trade and, in 1795, earned his freedom. Soon he had slaves of his own, named Brister and Boston, running the shop (whom he would eventually free). By the 1830s he would be worth over $86,000, having gained wealth through real estate and the produce of his three plantations. "He owned two or three plantations or farms," his contemporary Stephen Miller would write, "and a considerable number of slaves"—as many, at the peak of his career, as 167, most of whom worked his turpentine plantation.

The story is sometimes heard that J.C. Stanly purchased his slaves only for the purpose of teaching them a trade and then releasing them, but such was not the case at all.

He did free a few of the slaves he owned, and he purchased, then freed, a number of his own family members. It is curious to read the story of his starting a family. Since Kitty, his wife, was, early in their relationship, enslaved, he wound up having to purchase his own children, starting in 1800 with (yet another) John. In 1805 he purchased Kitty Green Stanly's freedom, along with that of his other children: Eunice, Catherine (also called Kitty) and Alexander.

A few slaves who were not relations, including Brister and Boston, also earned their manumission as a reward for hard work. One of his women earned independence as thanks for the care she'd given his wife in the long sickness leading to her death.

As to his slaves, Stanly was known for neither cruelty nor kindness. "In his treatment of his bondspeople, Stanly differed little from his white neighbors," historian Loren Schweninger wrote of him, then cited one of Stanly's acquaintances, Colonel John Whitford, as saying, "he was a 'hard task-master' who demanded long hours in the fields and 'fed and clothed them indifferently.'"

In one case a man named Edmond Pasteur had bought his freedom from Stanly. For the next six years Pasteur saved his money until he was able to purchase his wife, Dinah, and a child, Sarah, from his former master for $765 in 1820. He could not afford to purchase his son's freedom, however. Eight years later, Stanly sold that son to a man out of state. In another instance, Stanly held a man named Kelso in bondage, although he'd been born to a free woman (by law, making him a free man). The court ordered J.C. to set him free.

J.C. was apparently admired by his white neighbors as "a man of dignified presence" who "lived in fashionable style," his contemporary Stephen F. Miller would recall. "His sons and daughters were well educated, and always making a good appearance as bright mulattoes. No citizens of Newbern would hesitate to walk the streets with him." He was, Miller added, "uniformly courteous and unobtrusive," a suggestion that he was careful to show the deference expected of him from a community of whites who generally considered themselves his superiors in every way. It must have been a very fine line that he walked, maintaining both his dignity and his place in society.

The First Presbyterian Church in New Bern, of which the Stanlys were founding members. *Photo by the author.*

Stanly's wife, Kitty, was one of the founding members of New Bern's Presbyterian Church. Theirs was one of several families purchasing pews in 1822 as a means of raising funds to pay for the new church. The Stanly pews were located in the upper back corner of the balcony; they paid three hundred dollars for them. Their stylish home, on the corner of New and Hancock Streets, was within sight of the church.

He was careful to give his children a good education. His son, John Stewart, would own a store "well stocked with goods," Miller stated, doing "a heavy business" with customers who "had great confidence in his integrity."

Mr. Stanly was not a monster—he was a man of his society and times, accepting slavery as a fact of business and life. But the repeated story of his being a kind of Frederick Douglass of the South, buying up men only to train them and free them, is a fable. He did not entirely ignore his race; he often assisted newly freed blacks as their guardian and assisted the whites who wished to free them. But he obviously felt no compulsion to free his brethren on the basis of humanity or race: "Just like his white neighbors," Schweninger observed, "Stanly rose to a position of wealth and prestige through his ownership and use of slave labor."

William Gaston and John Stanly Jr.: As Alike as Fire and Ice

Mutt and Jeff. Lennie and George. Felix and Oscar. William and John.

You would have a difficult time finding a better list of friends whose natures were so apart.

William Gaston and John Stanly Jr. *did* have some things in common, these New Bern lawyers of the Antebellum: Both were staunch Federalists. John would serve in the assembly and rise to the position of congressman; William would serve as an assemblyman and become a state supreme court judge. While John's father was a Patriot who nearly lost his fortune for the cause, William's Patriot father died for it.

But where Stanly was a member of a well-to-do, powerful family, Gaston's mother—though admired—was relatively poor. Stanly was acceptably Protestant; Gaston, a devout Catholic, practiced a faith that by state constitutional law technically kept him from holding judicial office.

While William spoke with eloquence and compassion, Stanly was known for his sharp tongue, withering wit and powerful grudges. Stephen F. Miller, who was actually an admirer, recalled him as "a man of imperious temper" who, "as if not satisfied with having killed the father of Mr. Spaight in a duel twenty years before, he seemed to delight in torturing the son by look and gesture and intonations of his voice, when other methods were not devised…It was a fearful thing to incur his displeasure—it was next to annihilation." Miller also said that he never forgave his daughter, Elizabeth, for marrying the upstart officer Walker Keith Armistead (while visiting her father in 1817, she would give birth to one of Gettysburg's famous fallen, General Lewis Addison Armistead).

William Gaston's law office (now home of the New Bern Garden Club) stands in shadow of City Hall. *Photo by the author.*

Miller, who knew both men, described William's courtroom style thus:

> [He] *was diffident and when he first rose to address the court or jury, he trembled perceptibly, but in a few moments he was self-possessed, and commanded profound attention. In criminal cases…I have seen the tears roll down his face, while the jury and audience gave like tokens of sympathy. He increased the moral grandeur of his sentiments, and in the brilliance of his reasoning faculties as his argument progressed. He was uniformly respectful to suitors and witnesses, to the Court and to his brethren of the bar. When he closed a speech, the whole subject matter, both evidence and law had been exhausted by analysis and the mind rested with perfect confidence in the conclusions uttered.*

William was devoted to his family and to his faith. He hosted the town's Catholic services in his home. Miller, attending one service, reported, "There was a moral sublimity in the scene when Mr. Gaston partook of the sacrament in the midst of his Catholic brethren of foreign birth and humble pursuits."

Stanly was undoubtedly committed to his family, but his fiery temper shone through in his anger toward his daughter and his fatal advice to his brother to fight a duel.

In 1833 William Gaston became a supreme court judge of the state of North Carolina, although the state constitution stated that "no person who shall deny the truth of the Protestant religion…shall be capable of holding any place of trust or profit in the civil department within the state." William was able to sidestep the rule on the grounds that, though Catholic, he didn't really *oppose* Protestant views. He was the only Catholic at the constitutional convention of 1835, during which a new state constitution was written. William saw to it that the laws denying Catholics a place in civil service were eliminated.

But on another constitutional issue of civil rights, William lost. Prior to 1835, free blacks were allowed to vote in elections. This status had become continually worrisome to the whites of the state, especially after the 1831 Nat Turner rebellion in Virginia and the publication of David Walker's *Appeal*, which called for violent overthrow of white society by slaves.

Both William and John had received strong support from blacks. William, whose own experience with discrimination helped him feel their plight, and whose party was supported by freedmen, powerfully argued for their rights. He stated that denying their vote on the basis of color would degrade them—a remarkably broad-minded view for 1835—and suggested that letting them maintain their political voice would help keep them supportive of government and community. It would also, William said, be a positive influence on slaves.

Visions of blacks gaining a majority and electing black politicians, however, raised specters that won the day, and the Negro race found itself disenfranchised until the constitution of 1865.

William would marry twice—his first wife would live only a short time—and be the father of a son and two daughters. The second, Kate, "who lived almost next door to me," would die suddenly just as her father was preparing for the constitutional convention.

John's children would be numerous, including his eldest, an "idiot" who would live confined to his home until his death at age eighteen. Among his other children would be a Methodist minister and one son, Edward, who would be President Lincoln's choice as military governor during the Civil War. John's wife, Elizabeth Frank Stanly, a "shouting Methodist…without cultivation or opportunity" apparently brought more money than class into the family. "His nature did not harmonize with that of his wife," Miller would write. If they were alive today, perhaps his wall would feature a Monet garden scene; hers, a black velvet Elvis.

John Stanly would suffer a stroke while debating on the floor of the Senate in 1827, collapsing into the arms of fellow politician John Potter. Partially paralyzed, his career was over, and his finances (Miller would blame his sons; but John himself had much to do with it) would go to near ruin. His perpetual friend, William, who'd interceded with the governor on his behalf after the 1802 duel, came through again, saving his home from tax sale. After John died in 1834, William wrote a moving eulogy for him as "a truly great man," calling for remembrance of "his genius, his learning, his eloquence, his courtesy, his virtues, his personal character, and his public service."

William was a lover of poetry who would pen the state song. The state would ultimately honor him with a bust in Raleigh, and eventually name counties in both men's honor.

During their lives, William and John had a profound influence on New Bern as well as the state. In this town, the first half of the nineteenth century could be called "the Age of Stanly and Gaston."

Robert Hay: Swing Low, Sweet Carriage Maker

If there was a saint in New Bern, he was a Presbyterian.

Robert Hay was born in Gordon, Scotland, in 1754. He was already a middle-aged man when he first arrived in New Bern by the year 1800. But he would push on to the age of ninety-six and die one of the most beloved men in town.

He did nothing spectacular—he collected no fortune, held no office. He did not practice law, write books or shoot anyone in a duel. He simply arose each day, crossed the street to his shop and quietly built carriages. At the end of the day he walked back across the street and spent the evening with his family.

It was his character, not his actions, that brings him to our attention.

Robert's carriage shop was on grounds now fenced in as part of Tryon Palace. His home, a little federal side-hall he'd purchased for one thousand dollars around 1816, is also part of the Tryon Palace displays; you can go there today and tour it, visiting with character interpreters who act out the parts of the Hay family and friends.

A Presbyterian since his conversion at thirteen, Hay would always be known for his faith and his brogue. An acquaintance, Stephen F. Miller, described him thus: "A more devout or better man than Robert Hay has scarcely lived on earth. Leading a life of hard manual labor, his thoughts and communings seemed always to be of Heaven."

Hay's partner in the carriage business was Thomas Youle, another Gordon boy. In 1813 Youle, then forty-four, died and soon after, Hay, almost sixty, purchased his estate.

The same year his partner died, Robert Hay found himself under government suspicion for his British citizenship. The country was

A character interpreter's rendition of Robert Hay at the Hay House, Tryon Palace. *Photo by the author.*

embroiled in an unpopular war with England, and Hay was forced to register as an alien in the state.

In 1816 he apparently decided that sixty-two was a good age for starting a family. He married Nancy Carney, a woman quite a bit younger at twenty-five (though an "old maid" in the parlance of the day). Over the next several years, this pious old man would father a number of children: his eldest son William in 1817, Robert C. and Frances by 1820 and a last daughter, Mary, in 1834 (he was eighty!).

As devout as Hay was to the claims of Calvin, Calvin had made no claims, as yet, in New Bern. Probably carrying a Scottish dislike of anything Anglican, Robert aligned himself with the Methodist church in town. He was doubtless quite happy when as early as 1807, organizers began to meet to bring a Presbyterian church into town. Over the next few years, a number of families banded together to raise money to purchase land and then to raise a building. Robert's was one of thirteen founding families (along with, among others, John C. "Barber John" Stanly and his wife, Kitty). Robert was voted in as one of two chief elders.

The church Robert helped to found (and for which he would build some furniture) broke ground on June 9, 1819, and was dedicated in February 1822.

The prophet Daniel had nothing on Robert Hay when it came to prayer: every Sunday he would spend a fair amount of time in his closet, praying, along with gathering his family three times for prayer. His Godly communings in church were not always appreciated. "Mr. Hay prayed seventeen minutes with fervor!" a person in the congregation once reported, "A little too long for the congregation." At a service at another church, however, "Brother Hay prayed so fervently after sermon, as to cause groaning and some shouting among the blacks, and some knockings and amens among the whites."

He was a vigorous man, whose little house was usually filled with apprentices as well as his family and two slaves. His neighbor was John Jones, fellow founder of the Presbyterian church, a well-to-do distiller (of turpentine, not whiskey!). Robert both outlived and helped bury his younger neighbor: Jones would die at age seventy-six in 1840, and Robert, then eighty-six, would serve as a pallbearer to his grave.

A true Scotchman, Robert bought all things in cash. Never rich, he always pulled through until a fatal mistake in 1842 or '43 when he co-signed a note for his brother-in-law. The relative went bankrupt, and in April 1843, the courts put Hay's possessions up for a sheriff's sale to cover the debts.

The town reacted with horror. A prominent lawyer, George Attmore, came visiting to try and decide what could be done. Stephen Miller describes this little vignette:

> *Grieved, as were all men there, at this catastrophe to a man so blameless,* [Mr. Attmore] *visited Mr. Hay at his work-shop, where, bent with age, his face furrowed with cares and hair whitened by the snows of perhaps eighty winters, the good old Christian still wrought on, day by day. Greeting him sympathisingly the lawyer exclaimed: "This will never do, Mr. Hay. Your house must be saved; you cannot be turned out homeless in your old age, without a shelter for your family. We must devise ways and means to save your house, if nothing more." Leaning upon his implements of toil, with bent head and deeply thoughtful, the old man suddenly turned his face, full of emotion, towards his friend, exclaiming, in his strong Scotch accent, "Weel, George, my mon, save my hoose if ye can, George; but, mon, SAVE my conscience first!"*

When the sale took place, the residents of New Bern purchased everything in the house—then gave them back to Nancy Hay as a gift. Now in her name, there was nothing the law could do to seize them again.

As his vision clouded with age he spent much of the day pursuing the sun from window to window through the house, trying to keep the best light by which to read his Bible. "There he would sit for hours, with its full blaze upon its sacred pages," his pastor Daniel Stratton would report. "'If I were an idolator,' said he as his heart glowed with gratitude for the blessed light, 'I would worship the Sun.'"

He died on January 2, 1850. His pastor, Reverend Daniel Stratton was there to see him off. "A few moments before his death, when suffering from violent pain," the minister told the grieving congregation, "he exclaimed, 'I must be content; for "Blessed are the death that die in the Lord."'"

Drury Lacy:
Clerical Family Man

Drury Lacy is my favorite name in all of New Bern history: it suggests a character of dry wit and sophistication, while its similarity to "Drury Lane" oozes with fine irony. Drury Lane was, in that day, the very soul of carnality as London's Broadway; Drury Lacy, the very soul of spirituality as an educated and dedicated man of God.

But it is not his sermon notes and literate notations that get him into this collection; rather, it is his deep devotion to his family.

Drury was a Virginia boy, born in 1802 to a prominent clergyman and professor of the same name in Prince Edward County. A graduate of the Union Theologial Seminary in Virginia, he had never pastored a church before he came to New Bern to "try out" for the pulpit in September 1833. He impressed the congregation with his "emphatic" and "energetic" manner, according to church elder Elias Hawse. He charmed them even more with his brief (for that day) sermons: "45 minutes!!" was Hawse's comment for the next two sermons he gave—exclamation points included.

The congregation invited him to take the post, and on January 1, 1834, he began.

Drury brought with him his wife, Williana (known by friends as "Willie"), and a two-year-old daughter, Bessie. He would have a second child, James Horace Lacy, while still at New Bern in 1835.

The congregation received the young family with open arms and a furnished home. That house raised the ire of Willie's cousin back in Virginia, who would write to her, "You must have found it agreeable to go into a furnished house—when I first went home, the empty house looked so desolate that I was quite melancholy. Alas, for poor

Drury Lacy. *From* History of the Presbyterian Church, *published 1886.*

lawyers nobody cares how they fare. I reckon however that you do not need to be convinced of the advantage of being a minister's wife & therefore will not tell you of our troubles—how, we have to buy every thing & give twelve dollars a month for wood."

Hmmm. I thought she wasn't going to tell.

Drury frequently wrote to Willie, either while he was away on business or when she was off visiting family in Virginia. Those letters sparkle with the charm of his familial devotion. "My life is bound up in you, & the dear little ones," he would confess to her in June 1836.

"Remember what I whispered in your ear in the stage," he wrote another time. "Tell Bess I could read some of her little letter. 'Bessy Lacy'—she must learn to write sure enough & learn to spell & to read & to write me one little letter herself, in her own hand." He added for his infant son: "Horace, you little doggy, will you keep well and grow?

How many teeth have you my Son? You must learn to walk before Father sees you—and to say Pa-pa—Come!"

Drury kept a sense of humor about his loneliness when his family was away. "People say I have preached better since you have been gone," he wrote Willie in the same letter. "I don't know, but I have certainly studied harder, & made more diligent preparation—in fact, I have no heart to visit." He couldn't help but add a famous ministerial complaint, "…though they seem to think I have nothing else to do."

In another letter, his expression of loneliness for the family is almost pathetic: "We have had a very short life together, & I am for making the most of it—by keeping by my side, those I love best. Dear little children! Father would give anything to see you, & play with you, & kiss you a 100 times."

When it came to writing the rest of his family, however, his inkwell dried up. "Beg that cousin Drury will not forget to use his pen some times," begged the lawyer's wife—no doubt between bouts of counting out cash for the firewood. Another relative, writing to Willie, complained, "Tell Drury I wish he would not be so much like his brother in the *most* objectionable trait of his character…[in not] writing to his kinfolk."

Health—his family's and especially the town's—was always much on his mind. To hear Drury tell it, New Bern was all but a ghost town in the summer months. In June 1836 he wrote, "The people are deserting poor Newbern as usual, in every direction. Every vessel goes off with a full cargo of male & female. Every stage is crammed and the wealthiest are training their horses every day for their journey." Those who remained behind risked sickness and death—and, almost as bad, boredom in "this dull town." A number of his letters mention those who are sick and dying in the summer months.

During much of 1836 while Willie was away, Drury was quite ill. He spent several weeks at the homes of church friends, including a Mrs. Paskey and the home of John Jones, a turpentine distiller and church founder with whom he seemed to spend much time (Jones's house would, in the Civil War, become a temporary prison for the rebel spy Emeline Pigott). He did not want to worry his wife and he wrote her, trying to dispel her concern: "I hope there is nothing in their note that will become the least source of uneasiness to you my dear love, — I myself have felt no apprehension about the continuance of my disease, but have felt uneasy at your suspense, to know what has become of me.

"Be patient—be resigned—I trust I shall see you in 7 or 8 days—Do not be anxious—I tell you the simple naked truth—my writing shows that I can't be sick much. I have been sitting up (in bed) ever since breakfast talking with friends."

His penmanship in this note, far looser than his usual fluid style, must have given his wife pause despite his claims. He could not help but conclude with a note of concern for her: "Take care of yourself & the dear ones."

At the end of the year he left New Bern, taking a church in Raleigh. He had earlier stated his intent of "living and dying in the midst of you," but now, he told his congregation, "an imperious and overpowering sense of duty" drove him away.

As the years passed, he would serve variously as president of Davidson College, a home missionary in Virginia and as chaplain of the Confederate military hospitals in Raleigh during the Civil War.

Willie would die in 1846, and Horace in 1852 at the young age of seventeen. Both losses must have been devastating for Drury.

His New Bern congregation loved him, and Drury knew it. "I find every little occurrence that my dear family & my unworthy self are really beloved by affectionate friends here," he wrote Willie once. On his leaving, the church's trustees wrote to him of their "unabated affection and esteem for yourself and your family" and their regard for his "devotion to your calling…your labours amongst us."

A pastor couldn't ask for a better epitaph than that.

Part IV

The Civil War

Photo by the author.

Lewis Addison Armistead: New Bern's Famous Son

Call him "High Tide" Lew. He got farther into the Union ranks than any other Confederate during the Battle of Gettysburg. Unfortunately, he didn't get back out.

Waving his hat on the tip of his sword, calling encouragement to his men, he waded up Cemetery Hill into point-blank enemy fire that July 3, 1863, scaling the wall at "the Angle" and finally falling, shot three times. Two days later he died.

Armistead was the great-grandson of John Wright Stanly, grandson of John Stanly and the son of Elizabeth Stanly and War of 1812 veteran Walker Keith Armistead who, at the end of his life in 1845, was second in command of the U.S. Army. Lewis's uncle, George A. Armistead, by the way, was the defender of Fort McHenry on the day Francis Scott Key penned our national anthem.

Lewis Addison Armistead was a New Bern native, but more from accident than habitat: his parents were visiting Elizabeth's father in New Bern on February 18, 1817, when she went into labor and delivered him into the world. Once she recovered, the family went on to Upperville, Virginia, where he would be raised. This, perhaps, makes his the briefest residency of New Bern in this book and has caused some argument about his birthplace (nearly half the biographies I looked up on websites list his birthplace as that Virginia town).

In 1833, like most military-minded gentlemen, he entered West Point Academy. He had a hard time staying there. Illness caused him to resign once, and in 1836 he resigned for good over a headache. Not his own headache, but the one that his classmate Jubal Early had as a result of Lewis's breaking a mess plate over his head.

Lewis Addison Armistead.

You'd think that would have put an end to his career, but Lewis was fortunate in having a "hero" for a father and a powerful congressman and relative—Edward Stanly—back in New Bern. Strings were pulled, Pinocchio-style, and Lewis got his first commission in 1839. A second lieutenant in the Sixtieth U.S. Infantry, he waded about the swamps in Florida, evading gators and tracking down Seminole Indians, where his father, now a brigadier general, was in command.

In 1849 Lewis entered that training ground for the Civil War that we like to call the Mexican War. His bravery was rewarded with a captaincy and he spent the next few years recruiting in Kentucky.

These were not good years: in April of 1850 his young daughter, Flora Lee, died. His wife, Cecilia Love Armistead, died the same year. Following that old maxim of bad things happening in threes, the family home in Virginia burned to the ground in 1852, leaving little in its wake but ashes and memories. Attempting to rebuild his spiritual fortunes, Lewis married again, this time Cornelia Jameson. They had a child who, once again, died. Cornelia followed the same tragic suit and succumbed to cholera in 1855. Perhaps bad things come in fives.

On April 12, 1861, the guns of Charleston fired shots heard louder 'round America than those shots at Lexington had been heard 'round the world: two days later Fort Sumter fell. The Civil War had begun. Six weeks later, Lewis followed the path of most Virginians by resigning his commission. He was in Los Angeles at the time, visiting his old friend and fellow Mason, Winfield Hancock. He gave Hancock's wife Almira a prayer book, which was to be given to his family in the event of his death. They parted both friends and enemies, for Hancock would join the Union cause.

By the fall, Lewis had entered the Confederate Army as a major and, shortly after, was promoted to colonel and put in command of the Fifty-seventh Virginia. He saw action at Seven Pines and the Seven Days, a desperately fought battle in which Lee saved the Confederacy and extended the war. Armistead was personally involved in the bloodily repulsed attack on Malvern Hill, which concluded that affair.

In March he doubtless heard about New Bern's fall. While he had not lived there in years, he did have family there. One also wonders what he thought when he heard in May that Edward Stanly, the same uncle who'd helped salvage his military career, had become Lincoln's Union governor in North Carolina.

On April 1, 1862, Armistead became a brigadier general, was put in charge of a large brigade and assigned under General George Pickett. Fate was set.

In June 1863, Lee began his last march into northern territory. On July 1, he got into a firefight in the little shoemaking town of Gettysburg. Over the next three days, this would turn into the bloodiest and possibly the single most important battle of the Civil War. Pickett's Charge would be the climax of that great fight, and Lewis's brigade would march into the fight directly behind the brigades of James Kemper and Richard Garnett. There was a huge and interesting irony here: He had begun the war with a party at the home of his friend, Winfield Hancock. Here he would end it by attacking Hancock's lines at the top of Cemetery Hill.

Now, lying wounded in the midst of the wounded and dead of his own and his friend Hancock's brigades, Lewis learned from a Union captain whose line he had attacked. Hancock could not visit him, he was told, because he, too, had been wounded in the fight—at almost the same moment as Lewis. "Tell General Hancock from me," Lewis begged the captain, "that I have done him and you all a grave injustice."

Armistead's brief victory is sometimes called the High Tide of the Confederacy: he got farther in the lost cause than any other, paid the final price and became an example of "brother against brother" and "friend against friend." It is unlikely that many Southerners, however, would consider his final effort any kind of injustice at all.

The Forty-fourth Massachusetts: An Occupation Thanksgiving

In 1863, old Honest Abe (or that "Ape Abe" if you were a southron) declared the first official Thanksgiving.

But the soldiers of the Forty-fourth Massachusetts, a nine-month regiment occupying New Bern, held a huge Thanksgiving celebration a good year earlier. That's a Yankee for you: always jumping the gun.

We have some remarkably good sources for their celebration, including a list of foods and a litany of speakers, provided by a number of soldiers whose writing appears in books and published and unpublished letters—especially those of Private Henry Clapp, William Hedge and Corporal Zenas T. Haines (who wrote for the *Boston Herald*).

The Forty-fourth was an elitist company of sorts, made up primarily of high-society Bostonians (among them the brother of Henry James and the founder of the Natural Museum of New York) who had signed up for a nine-month stint. A kind of fraternity ("They should be drilled in Latin!" one observer scoffed) who spent a lot of time indulging in dances and shows, they also left their trail of blood in a pair of fall and winter campaigns.

Haines, in his newspaper report of December 1, claimed, "Thanksgiving Day…was duly celebrated by the Massachusetts troops at this post. It would not have been observed with more feeling and *éclat* by the same individuals at home."

William Hedge, a First Lieutenant of Company C, wrote home that "many are the preparations being made for a New England Thanksgiving dinner. Bob our Contraband—a burly young fellow of twenty—has just come in with eyes grinning…while in his hands he holds two pair of lively-cackling young hens, which he is to fatten…"

James Bruerton of the same company described the company's veritable feast, served up by the corporals: "There was then on the table, soft bread, hard bread, butter and apple sauce. The first article which the corporals had the pleasure of handing to us was stewed oysters and I noticed that three plates full disappeared down my throat, together with…any quantity of apple sauce, just in time for the roast beef…of course I tried some of that together with sweet and irish potatoes." Apples and a "tip top" plum pudding rounded off the dinner. Trout, ginger snaps, onions, goose and cigars were devoured in other meals.

Soldiers on the march could clean out the countryside, making for a sparse Thanksgiving for citizens. *Courtesy Fred Smith Collection, Tryon Palace Historic Sites and Gardens.*

Company A featured a full-blown program with original music and a speech by A.S. Bickmore, who would soon die in battle at Whitehall. At least two other companies broke up into squads and dined in style in New Bern homes and eateries.

Company F was best known for its airs and literary aplomb, and it is Henry Clapp, a somewhat egotistical but eloquent writer, who gives us some of the most complete pictures of the Forty-fourth's celebration (his collected letters, *Letters to the Home Circle*, is currently in print). In one letter home he talks about the struggle of finding turkeys. "They were hard to get for few were in the market. I take a great deal of pride and pleasure in the fact that I went down to the town with Corporal Denny before daylight last Monday morning and was successful in getting *Twenty five*."

Company F also celebrated with orators and toasts while other companies put together large evening entertainments. Another regiment, the Massachusetts Fifth, celebrated the day with a mock parade, wearing their clothes inside out.

And the Confederates? They had reason for thanks: General Lee was making remarkable progress in Virginia and the watershed events of Vicksburg and Gettysburg were still eight months away. Still, the war had not gone well in North Carolina, with every coastal town but Wilmington controlled by Union blue.

General S.G. French, Confederate commander of the Department of North Carolina, celebrated his Thanksgiving by writing an angry letter to General Foster, the Union commander in New Bern, complaining of "many wanton acts of destruction of private property and many depredations…committed by the troops under your command" earlier that month. This no doubt resulted in many a secessionist son's and daughter's meager Thanksgiving. Foster vehemently denied French's charges, but the letters of his men written during that time suggest the good General Foster "doth protest too much." "The men foraged with all their might," Clapp himself wrote. "As we marched along they ran out into all the houses and cleaned out every thing eatable, alive and dead."

Another letter writer of the Forty-fourth, Private James Bruerton of Company C, described another incident on the march: "An old man & his son with several women were in the house, the son we took prisoner and confiscated his horse and wagon. The women bellowed some and one asked what she should do without her sweetheart. As soon as the cavalry arrived they went down to the house and the way the chickens, hens, turkeys, ducks, honey sweet potatoes & etc. disappeared was a caution."

One can find numerous, hilarious accounts of soldiers taking animals, vegetables, goods and honey (hilarious, that is, if you are not the farmer watching your family's sustenance disappear down the throats of your already well-stocked enemy). Some homes were suspiciously set ablaze. And Clapp bragged in a letter home about a massive "quarto law volume" to which he helped himself while on the march. None of this was robbing civilians, of course: it was war.

Regarding the celebration of an elaborate Thanksgiving in an occupied town, we have good witness. Regarding the "Secesh" celebration—at least where the ravaging armies had touched—we can well imagine. It is an interesting picture to meditate upon as we ogle our sweet potato soufflé and dressing this next official Thanksgiving Day.

William Henry Singleton: Slave to Freedman and Civil War Hero

You've probably heard of Robert Gould Shaw and the Fifty-fourth Massachusetts, the black regiment that stamped itself with glory in a disastrous fight at Fort Wagner in 1863. The Fifty-fourth had New Bern connections, for Colonel Shaw scoured this town to find officers for his new regiment. Among them was Wilkie James, brother of the author Henry James; Wilkie would serve the new regiment with distinction.

But we're here to talk about William Henry Singleton, not Wilkie or Bob.

For New Bern was not only recruiting officers for black regiments. It was recruiting *men*.

Since the town's fall in early '62, New Bern had become a Mecca for freedom-seeking slaves. The town's population doubled and tripled as "contraband" flooded its streets. For the most part, they didn't simply hang about. Letters and regimental histories of the day are filled with commentary about the services newly freed blacks gave: cooking, cleaning and otherwise hiring themselves out for duties to officers and in the camps.

But not every freedman was ready to simply become servile-for-pay. Witness the story of the remarkable slave, William Henry Singleton.

Singleton was born about 1843 in New Bern, like so many, the son of an African American woman and a white man. When he was five his master, John H. Nelson, sold him to a woman in Atlanta. Henry's—he went by his middle name—new owner was a woman who ran what he called a "slave farm," purchasing young slaves and raising them until they could be sold for a good price. "I did not like the idea of leaving my mother and my brothers," he would recall. "I did not like my mistress, either." Made to sleep on a dirt floor "like a dog" and frequently abused with whippings, he ran away two years later and returned to the Singleton plantation.

A soldier's drawing of a freed slave in New Bern. *Courtesy Fred Smith Collection, Tryon Palace Historic Sites and Gardens.*

As he grew he dreamed of freedom and resented his bondage. "In the country of the Declaration of Independence," he would later write, "I was born a slave, for I was a black man…in the eyes of the law I was but a thing. I was bought and sold…Once I was whipped simply because it was thought I had opened a book."

When the Civil War broke out, Henry sought a position as servant to Samuel Hymans, a local West Point student who'd organized a company of soldiers for the Second North Carolina regiment (the Elm City Rifles). It wasn't so much admiration for Hymans as it was a bid for freedom: "I wanted to learn how to drill," Henry wrote.

While camped in Kinston, shortly after the fall of New Bern in March 1862, Henry saw his chance and fled to the new Mecca where he spent a day or two under guard while the Yankees tried to determine if he was a legitimate runaway or a spy. Soon he was serving as an unarmed scout during one of General Burnside's near-futile attacks on Kinston. A horse was shot out from under him and, unnerved by the event, he told the colonel he served that he would not help again unless he was armed. "We never will take niggers in this army to fight," the man replied.

Furious, Henry demanded his pay—five dollars—then hired out the city's A.M.E. Zion Church and started a recruiting drive for colored soldiers. "I secured the thousand men," he would write. "They appointed me as their colonel and I drilled them with cornstalk for guns."

It was not an official position—African Americans would never be allowed to serve as commissioned officers in that war. Henry tried to convince General Burnside to put the regiment into service, but he refused.

Still, it was through Burnside that Henry claimed to have met Abraham Lincoln, who had come, he said, for a conference call. "This is the little fellow who got up a colored regiment," Burnside told the president. "President Lincoln shook hands with me and said, 'It is a good thing. What do you want?'" He pressed his desire for the regiment's service, but the president was not quite ready for a colored force. But "keep your men together," he advised. "There may be a chance for you."

This particular memory was probably invented; there is no record of Lincoln's visiting New Bern.

Their chance arrived when the Emancipation Proclamation made Henry and his men officially free; on May 28, 1863, James Beecher, brother of the abolitionist preacher Henry Ward Beecher, took over Henry's regiment as colonel and Henry himself was made a sergeant in Company G. He was, he boasted, the first black man to be accepted for federal service and the only one to raise an entire regiment during the Civil War. Named the First North Carolina Colored Regiment, it was later renamed the Thirty-fifth Regiment, United States Colored Troops.

His regiment would see service in South Carolina, Florida and Georgia, and Henry would be wounded at his regiment's own Fort Wagner. On February 20, 1864, the largest battle in Florida took place when 5,500 federal troops attempted to burn railroad tracks and were fought off by 5,000 Confederates at Olustee, near Jacksonville. The Union was routed, suffering 37.5 percent casualties; the Thirty-fifth lost 22 men killed, 131 men wounded and 77 missing—undoubtedly to inglorious ends. Though a total defeat, Henry's regiment had performed "splendidly," according to an observing officer of the Sixth Massachusetts Volunteers.

Following the war, Henry was converted to religion in an A.M.E. Zion church. He tried to settle in New Bern, but death threats from the Ku Klux Klan forced him to leave his hometown forever.

"My life since the war has been the ordinary life of the average man of my race," he wrote in his published memoir in 1922. "I have not so many accomplishments to boast of, but I have done the best that I could to prove myself worthy of being a free man."

What more could one ask?

Emeline Pigott: Spy in a Hoop Skirt

Hoop skirts were the greatest undercover weapon of the Civil War. After all, what can't you hide in a hoop skirt? A Napoleon cannon, perhaps; an Abrams tank. That about covers it.

Emeline Pigott would make fine use of that weapon in the dark last years of the war. She was one of those freedom-loving Sagittarius types, born December 15 as an early Christmas present to her folks in Harlowe Township, Carteret County, in 1836. She grew up just north of Morehead City. In those days it could more appropriately be called Morehead One Horse Town.

Living at little Crab Point, we are told that twenty-five-year-old Emeline looked across the creek that flowed past her home into the camps of the Twenty-sixth North Carolina. Her heart went out to the boys of the Confederacy and she began to tend their sick and wounded—some in her own home. The officers had an eye for the young belle and invited her to dances and balls, but Emeline had come upon a young private named Stokes McRae whom she loved with all the passion of her age and era. Stokes loved her, too, and they became engaged. She sewed him a Confederate flag out of silk, we are told, mounted on a gold staff. The quality of its stuff sounds a bit legendary, but the event no doubt took place. He carried the flag proudly and doubtless steeped with pleasure in his fellow soldiers' jealous gazes.

In early 1862 it was becoming obvious that coastal North Carolina was in for a serious blow—not from any hurricanes or nor'easters, but from the approaching flotillas of that bushy scion of mutton chops, General Ambrose Burnside. On March 14, he landed in force at the Officer's Club at Cherry Point Marine Air Corps Station—no, the base was not yet there, and neither was the club. Perhaps fleeing their advance, Emeline was in New Bern while Stokes crouched in the

Jones House in 1862. Today it is a gift shop of Tryon Palace Historic Sites and Gardens. *From the Fred Smith Collection. Courtesy Tryon Palace Historic Sites and Gardens.*

trenches awaiting an onslaught that the meager Confederate force had no hope of holding off.

The line fell; Stokes lost his flag in his regiment's retreat. When the news of disaster reached town, Emeline watched as citizens and soldiers alike fled for the train station, clambering onto any cars rolling out of town. She did not leave until the last trains chugged out, sharing a flat car with wounded soldiers. It must have been some ride, hearing the clack-clack of the tracks in tune to the contrapuntal moans and cries of bloody men. Her heart went to them again and, remaining in Kinston for some weeks, she nursed the men to health.

Meanwhile, Stokes and his regiment headed into Virginia. Except for a brief flirtation with Union regiments in and about Little Washington, he would not visit North Carolina again: in July 1863, he met his fate at Gettysburg. Heartbroken, Emeline, now in Concord, vowed to dedicate herself to her lover's cause.

Some women cropped their hair and signed up to fight, but Emeline was perhaps too feminine for that. Instead, she and her brother-in-law, Rufus Bell, returned to her home near Morehead City. There, she pulled a Mata Hari before Mata Hari was born, entertaining Union men who occupied her home, charming information from them and slipping it beyond Union lines to Confederate agents. She recruited local fishermen who sold their catches to Union ships and reported to her names and numbers. She also took to personally carrying contraband items to Rebels—food, clothing and medicine that, for the Rebels, was in short supply. On some trips her bloomers bloomed with as much as thirty pounds of items for the South.

It was in early 1865 that she convinced some Northern men to write information for her to deliver across the lines. She tucked the paper into her dress, against her heart and, with Rufus, began her trip across the lines. But by this time, the Union was looking at the pair and smelling rats. Both were arrested but Rufus, being found with empty pockets, was released. It was trickier to determine what to do with Emeline, who stood in a severely polite society of men who just knew they had a woman whose skirts were laden with booty—but not a man among them was willing to search her. A black woman was found, but the genteel Southern lady would not allow a daughter of Africa to touch her. While an alternative was sought, Emeline ate the document she carried and tore some personal letters to bits.

When the search was finally performed, she was discovered to be carrying an enormous quantity of items from clothing to combs to boots. Perhaps there was a sink in there, possibly a manual for an Abrams tank.

She was caught, red-faced and red-handed, as a spy. By law she could have been hanged for her crime. For a time she was imprisoned in an upper chamber of the John Jones House (now the gift shop and offices at Tryon Palace Historic Sites and Gardens). Was she brought to trial? By one account, Emeline contacted some influential New Bern men and presented them with the dirt she had on them: if she went down, she said in effect, *they* went down. The trial never took place.

By another account she was tried and sentenced to death—but for reasons unknown the sentence was never carried out.

Whichever case it might have been, she was freed before the war ended and returned to her home on Crab Point. We can be sure she was on a do-not-visit list for all Union men.

Emeline lived out a full life, telling her stories of derring-do. She died May 26, 1919, at the age of eighty-two and lies at rest today in the family cemetery on the north side of Calico Creek.

One wonders what she might have slipped into that coffin with her.

The Sisters of Mercy: Good Habits to Have About

Historian Ellen Ryan Jolly called them "Nuns of the battlefield." It puts a remarkable image in my mind, of a Monty Python routine in which the Sisters of Saint Joan lead a charge into German cannons (or, perhaps, German canons?). The whole idea takes a lot of Gaul, I suppose. Or Bull.

Probably more than a few eyebrows were raised when, in Beaufort in July of 1862, the steamer *Cahawba* arrived, spewing out a line of nuns swaddled in yards of heavy black fabric. They probably smelled horsy, having traveled a couple of hundred nautical miles in the company of five hundred cavalry horses. With these Sisters of Mercy was Mother Mary Madelene Tobin, head of their order, and their Hungarian chaplain, Father Bruhl.

They came bearing bandages and good will. Of course, they had entered a military town, with military hospitals run by military men. Mother Mary knew her work was cut out for her. The hospital in town was an old hotel, its walls stained with soldiers' blood. The women looked about in consternation: convalescing soldiers—the closest thing there to a nurse—limped among the less fortunate patients in dankness and filth.

The sisters quickly declared war, demanding (and receiving) medicines and supplies from General Foster, head of military operations in North Carolina. By force of will, Mother Mary convinced Dr. John Upham, head of the hospital, to surrender the running of everything but the medical department to her.

The heat—possibly exacerbated by their hot clothes—rapidly took its toll. Four nuns, including Mother Mary, succumbed to sickness; they were shipped north to recover (one, Sister Paul Lennon, would die of her illness). To Dr. Upham's amazement, Mother Mary named their cook, Sister Augustine MacKenna, to replace her.

In October, General Foster ordered them moved to New Bern, where he vacated his quarters in the Stanly House for their accommodation. "We were agreeably surprised at the aspect of the Stanley House," Sister Augustine would write. The yard was full of periwinkle, cedars and mockingbirds. Tickled with their elaborate surroundings, the nuns did all they could to make the place plain. But you can only do so much to quash beauty: "The magnificent drawing room in the Mansion is now our chapel," Sister Augustine continued, "Gorgeous roses cluster around and climb into the windows and mocking-birds fluttering through the branches serenade the Sisters at their prayers, while two majestic trees, 'The Pride of India'—stand sentinels of honor before the entrance."

Jammed to the eaves with soldiers and ringed by forts, New Bern was rarely attacked. But endless marches and military expeditions, along with the usual malarial fevers and choleras kept the nuns busy.

Susan Messinger, a Boston woman who followed the Massachusetts Forty-fifth Regiment into town, seemed particularly interested in the sisters. "I saw them constantly," she would write for the *Regimental Record*, "and can testify to their constant, unselfish devotion to those brought to their charge."

Messinger stated that the nuns drew heavily from government stores for supplies, but also were "dependent upon contribution for all delicacies. They told me the 'sanitary' was very liberal but 'oh, the need so great!'"

Messinger related the story of "One dear young fellow, who was almost reverenced by the doctors and nurses for his patience and fortitude, [and] looked up into the sweet face of Mother Augustine, as she bent over to minister or soothe the dear boy, and said, 'Mother, thank you, Mother.' And with such an ineffable smile of peace. We could never tell if in his delirium he thought it was his own Mother, but the peace on the boy's face showed what the nurse had been to him. His sickness was short and death came just before the father reached Newberne."

The Goldsboro campaign of 1862 resulted in a large number of wounded pouring in for the sisters' care. They arrived in sad condition, most of them a good eight days after the battle, having

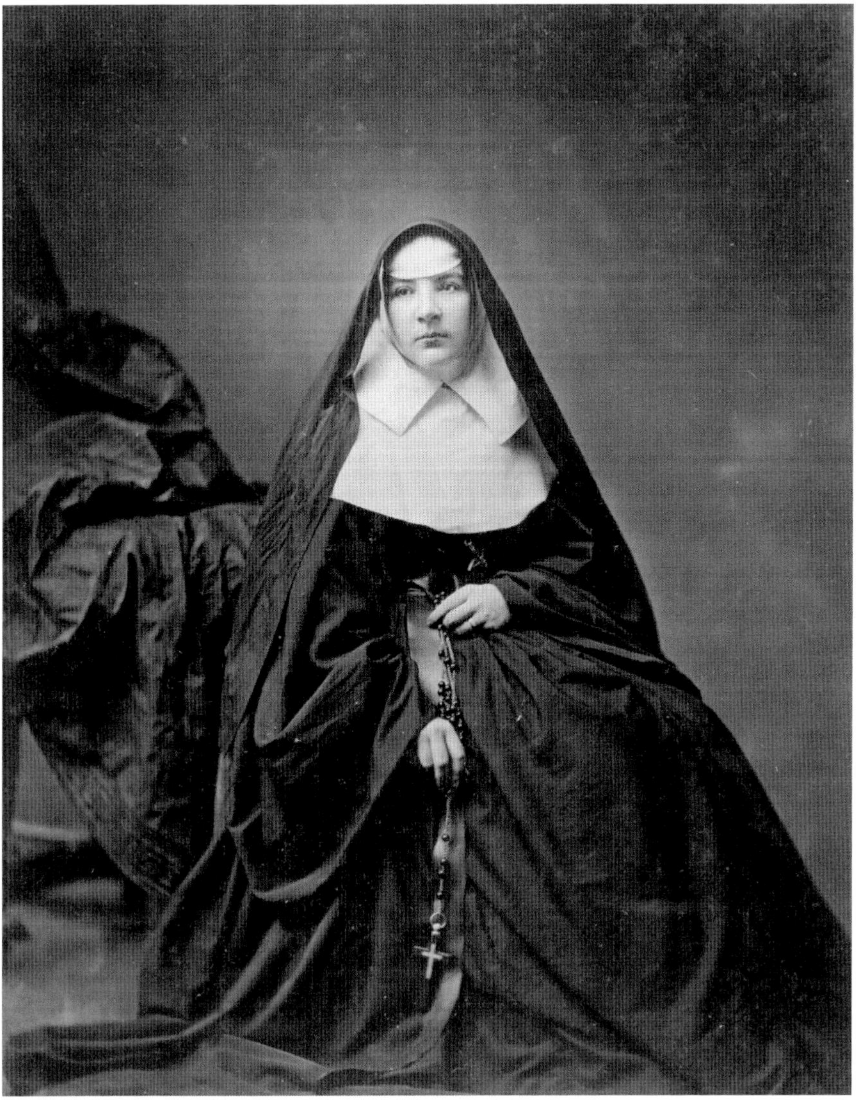

Sister Joseph, photographed in Beaufort in 1862. *Library of Congress, Prints and Photographs Division.*

been uncared for during most of that time. The sisters had very little in the way of linen with which to bandage them.

Long marches could sometimes bring a toll along with sickness and battle wounds. Such was the case of David Brout, related in Ryan's *Nuns of the Battlefield*:

> *Sister Ignatius Grant…noticed that he kept moving his feet in a distressed way, so she uncovered them to seek the cause. What was her horror to discover that he still had his boots on and that they seemed ready to burst. She asked a couple of soldiers to come with knives and remove them piece by piece. This they did with great difficulty, and then alas! It was found that the legs had actually burst open and the boots were filled with clotted blood. The doctors were summoned and had great trouble in staunching the blood flow and in tying up the arteries. The poor lad died in great agony the next day. He was the victim of a forced march…*

The Goldsboro campaign was followed in December and January by a brief spate of yellow fevers, but the remainder of winter and early spring of 1863 was quiet. By April the sisters found their hospital halls as empty of patients as they once had been of bandages. Regimental hospitals, alone, were apparently able to keep up with the work and so, on May 10, accompanied by four Negro girls, they returned to their convent in New York, this time without the accompanying music provided by five hundred cavalry horses.

The order still runs today, with its emphasis on medical and social care.

Perhaps their material poorness is still compensated for by their patients' love and appreciation. As Ms. Messinger said, "The 'sisters' were interested in all who came under their care…It mattered little what their creed—the loving service was complete and cheerful."

James Walker Hood: A.M.E. Zion's Man of God

James Walker Hood grew up loving Jesus and freedom.

Like many carpetbaggers, he was born and raised in a Pennsylvania town, and he took advantage of the Civil War to settle himself for business in an occupied Southern city: New Bern. But he wasn't a carpetbagger—he was black, and his business had little to do with financial gain.

He was born in a southeastern corner of Pennsylvania in 1831, the son of Levi and Harriet Walker Hood, a deeply religious family that helped found a colored Methodist church that preached abolition. Levi, a minister, had not known slavery, but he knew all about it. Emancipation was such a motivating force in his life that even apprenticeship was against his belief: it bound a young man too closely to his master.

James received minimal formal training early in life, most of it by his mother. But he learned quickly, and by 1843 was giving abolition speeches. He was also "saved" as a boy, at age eleven, and believed in his calling as a pastor from that early age. At one point in his childhood, James was kidnapped by white slavers, but escaped them before he could be shipped south.

Much of his childhood was spent in the company of Quakers, a predominantly white group—the first group to send ministers into North Carolina, by the way—a group known for its pacifistic and abolitionist ways. The Quakers were behind a significant part of the Underground Railroad.

In 1852 the young man, by now studying for ministry, met and married Hannah Ralph, although she died just three years later of consumption. He married again in 1858.

James Walker Hood. *Courtesy St. Peter's A.M.E. Zion Church.*

In 1860, a few months after John Brown's body began a-moldering in the grave, John Walker Hood was ordained a deacon in the A.M.E. Zion Church. This black denomination had been founded in 1796 in New York City; within two years, he was elected elder.

By now the Civil War was raging; in New Bern, one Massachusetts soldier wrote, the streets were full of soldiers and Negroes, having become a Mecca for slaves seeking freedom. The harvest was ripe for a missionary movement among the population.

But the time was not yet ripe for James: though he'd become a missionary, his first field was north to the forested realms of Nova Scotia. There, he founded a black community and, in the midst of

"Hardshell Baptists," a small Methodist enclave. Midway through 1863 he was called to Hartford, Connecticut. From there, the church turned its eyes to North Carolina, and James's true life calling began.

He arrived in New Bern late that year. Ringed by forts, its rivers bobbing with gunboats while its fields were flecked with the barracks and tents of numerous regiments. This was a town well protected from Confederate, pro-slavery intrusion. James was probably amazed at the huge number of blacks—freedmen and former slaves, semi-educated or completely illiterate—who roamed the streets.

In New Bern, a town noted for its disproportionately large population of free blacks, several churches already held black memberships—such as the Presbyterian Church, which boasted African Americans among its founders. Andrew's Chapel—today it is named St. Peter's—was an all-black congregation that had been meeting since 1839. Shortly after the town's fall, J.E. Round, a white minister of the Methodist Episcopal (M.E.) denomination, had been preaching and teaching Sunday school.

Though he contracted small pox the day after his arrival (the military temporarily shut down religious services in an attempt to control the outbreak), James was able, with the help of former New Bern resident and current bishop Christopher Rush to convince the people to switch over to the all-black denomination. Reverend Round, who'd arrived at the church with Secretary of War Edwin M. Stanton's blessings, naturally wanted to keep this congregation within the M.E. fold, however. Though predominantly white, the Methodist Episcopals boasted a large black membership up north. He used this, along with Stanton's blessings and a kind of squatter's rights for himself, as a means of demanding the congregates for his own.

It took some significant pulling of strings, but James appealed to Stanton and convinced him to let the local congregation make its own choice. Stanton relented, and for the next three years James pastored Andrew's.

But James was not happy just climbing into a pulpit once a week. With the end of the war came the beginnings of reconstruction: with the happiness of freedom, there was a race to keep the emancipated down. A new state constitution gave the blacks the right to vote, but a new order, the Ku Klux Klan, arose to keep the majority of those voters in their homes, and to chase the "nigger-loving" carpetbaggers back North. In 1865, as the new state constitution was being drawn up, James presided over the first statewide political convention for blacks, demanding civil and political rights for his people. He would represent his district in the 1868 constitutional convention, pushing for education and homesteading provisions.

From New Bern he would move on to pastor in Fayetteville and then Charlotte; afterward he would be named bishop and, in that position, travel the country and even the world. He would continue to preside over a number of annual denominational conferences and write the first published collections of sermons by a black preacher in America. He would pen another four histories and theological works. He would also continue his activity within the Republican party of North Carolina and help establish Livingstone College in Salisbury, presiding over its board for thirty years.

Widowed a second time, he married Keziah P. McCoy, a twenty-seven-year-old widow, in 1877, when he was forty-six. He would live until October 30, 1918 when he "finished the race" in Fayetteville, a man well-used and using his time quite well.